C000225009

Walking the Howgills

Mary Welsh

with illustrations by

Christine Isherwood

Copyright © Mary Welsh, 1998

All Rights Reserved. No part of this publication may be reproduced, stored in a retrieval system, or transmitted in any form or by any means – electronic, mechanical, photocopying, recording, or otherwise – without prior written permission from the publisher.

Published by Sigma Leisure – an imprint of
Sigma Press, 1 South Oak Lane, Wilmslow, Cheshire SK9 6AR, England.

British Library Cataloguing in Publication Data
A CIP record for this book is available from the British Library.

ISBN: 1-85058-600-4

Typesetting and Design by: Sigma Press, Wilmslow, Cheshire.

Cover illustration: The River Rawthey below the Cross Keys Inn

Maps and illustrations: Christine Isherwood

Printed by: MFP Design and Print

Disclaimer: the information in this book is given in good faith and is believed to be correct at the time of publication. No responsibility is accepted by either the author or publisher for errors or omissions, or for any loss or injury howsoever caused. Only you can judge your own fitness, competence and experience.

Contents

Location Map

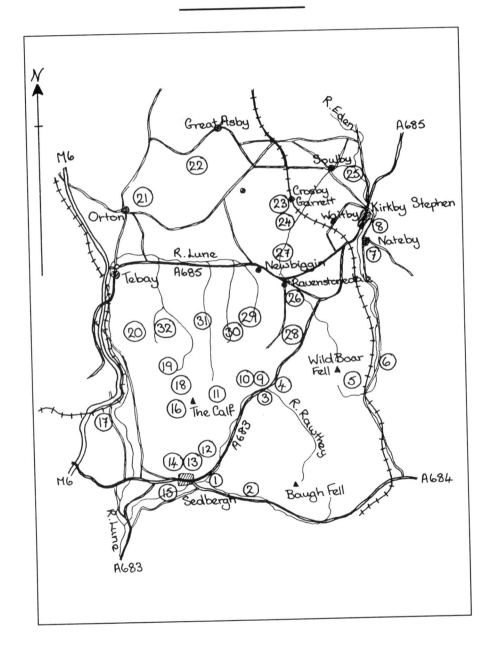

Walk 1: Sedbergh – Dowbiggin

Straight Bridge – Burntmill Bridge – Ghyllas –
Hebblethwaite Hall – Sarthwaite – Fellgate – Sweet Hill –
Hallbank – Garsdale Bridge – Straight Bridge

Start/finish: A large lay-by just before Straight Bridge on the south side of A683, a mile east of Sedbergh (GR 677927).

Type of walk: A glorious 5-mile country walk through the hidden charms of Dowbiggin. Very narrow lanes pass between tall hedges, quiet farms snuggle at the foot of the fells or tuck into folds in rolling pastures and spectacular tree-lined gills hide dancing becks. The return is made alongside the surging River Clough, where you are likely to see several pairs of dippers, and to the charming Garsdale Bridge.

Map: OS Outdoor Leisure 19 Howgill Fells and Upper Eden Valley

The Walk

Walk on from the lay-by to cross Straight Bridge over the River Rawthey. Take the second narrow lane on the right, signposted Dowbiggin, and walk on for 150 metres. Turn left into a delightful, easy-to-miss, hedged green lane. At its end, bear right to walk a loop of the old road and to cross Burntmill Bridge. Pause here to enjoy the hurrying Hebblethwaite Hall Gill beck as it races over two weirs. Look for the waterwheel on the old mill and the millstones incorporated into the hard-standing in front of the dwelling.

Climb the steps to join the A-road and walk on for 275 metres along the wide grass verge to take a footpath on the right, signposted Hebblethwaite Hall. Climb the steepish steps to a stile and go on through oak and rhododendrons. Stroll the metalled track and just before a farm, Ghyllas, take the waymarked stile on the left.

Climb the next waymarked stile and carry on, with a pleasing

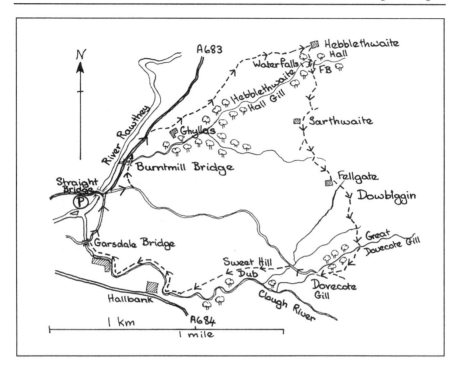

view, left, of the Howgills. Pass through the next gate and look for the signpost in the hedge on your left. Here leave the pasture to join the farm track and turn right for Hebblethwaite Hall.

Pause by the farm to look at the attractive cluster of buildings. In the 18th century this was the site of a busy mill, employing many workers from Sedbergh in the manufacture of woollen goods. Later it produced bobbins.

To continue the walk, take the stone-stepped stile in the wall on the right, south, just before the hall. Walk ahead to a stile into the stunning Hebblethwaite Gill, where the Woodland Trust welcomes visitors to walk in the wood. Follow the steps, which drop steeply right and then left, to cross a footbridge over the chuckling beck. The path continues just as steeply uphill, beneath tall beech. Once out of the gill, walk right to peer over the fence to a delightful waterfall, where the beck rages over great slabs of rock.

Walk uphill over the rough pasture to the top right corner to pass through two fine gateposts. Turn right to stroll a grassy track beside a straggly alder and hawthorn hedge; in the past hawthorn trees were used as waymarkers for packhorse routes.

The track goes on through two gates and then swings left, with the wall to your left and Sarthwaite, a deserted farm with a pleasant traditional porch, to your right. Go on along the grassy track to pass through a gate, then follow the track to a gap stile to the left of a gate in the wall.

Dipper

Here the way divides, one path going through the gate towards a large barn, the other, the one you should follow, passing through the gap stile and continuing across the pasture to a turf bridge, hidden in the bottom of a grassy gill. Once beyond, bear half left towards Fellgate Farm, set among trees.

Pass through the gate and, with the farmhouse to your right, swing left to a gate onto the lower slopes of Baugh Fell, where you turn right. (Here you are likely to encounter several rather noisy dogs.) Follow the track parallel with the wall to your right and stay with it as it continues its winding way towards a small building with a chimney beside a sheepfold. Make time for another pause here to savour the view of the Howgills stretching from Wandale to Winder.

Stride on, with a sturdy wall to your right, to cross Great Dovecoat Gill on convenient boulders. Pause midway and look upstream to see where the beck tumbles gently through the quiet fells, its humpy banks like miniature Howgills. Then look right to the wooded gorge – here the beck descends noisily and is quickly lost to sight in the great cleft of Dovecote Gill.

You are now on the edge of the Dent Fault and below your feet sandstone has ceased, to be replaced by limestone. Look for the many shake holes beside the path. The fault is a major fracture of the earth's crust, which formed some 290 million years ago. At this locality and at that time, the rocks of the Lake District were lifted one and a half miles above those of the Pennines.

Turn right and follow the wall on your right. Continue on the track and when opposite a limekiln on your left, pass through the gate on your right. Follow the clear, curving, grassy way as it comes close to a wall on your right. Away to your left is a signpost which directs you in the direction of Dowbiggin Lane, the grassy track you are walking is heading in that direction, taking the easiest route over the rough pasture, with the lovely wooded gill just over the wall.

The track, now a sunken path, is wooded on both sides. Go on to a T-junction of paths, where you take, on the left, the ladderstile signposted Hallbank. Stride ahead over Sweet Hill to a gated stile and head on to take the next stile in a fence. A third stile is set in a hawthorn hedge. Beyond, stroll a terrace-like path above the River Clough, from where you are likely to see dippers.

Ignore the footbridge on the left, continue to the end of the pasture and take a stile at the point where the river makes a sharp right turn.

Stroll the glorious stiled way, with the Clough, to your left, racing through its alder-lined banks. On the opposite bank you can see an extensive mill, once it wove cloth and today a part of it is used for manufacturing walking fleeces.

Continue towards the charming Garsdale Bridge. Climb the stone steps in the wall to join a narrow lane. Turn right and walk the flowery lane, which is even narrower than the one taken at the outset of your walk, to join the A683. Turn left and cross Straight Bridge to rejoin your car.

Garsdale Mill

Walk 2: Garsdale – Geological trail, Longstone Common, above Sedbergh

Longstone Common – Danny Bridge – River Clough – New Bridge – Aye Gill – lower slopes of Baugh Fell – Danny Bridge – Sedgwick geological trail – Longstone Common

Start/finish:	Large parking area, 2½ miles from Sedbergh, on the A684, the road to Hawes (GR 695912).
Type of walk:	This delightful 6½ mile walk takes you into Garsdale alongside a placid stretch of the tree-lined Clough River. It is generally well waymarked and stiled. The return is over pastures and then along a narrow gated lane, below the lower slopes of Baugh Fell, giving you grand views down into the river valley. The walk ends with an optional extra of following, beside a much more petulant Clough, the Sedgwick geological trail. Numbered posts indicate points of interest from where you can see the rock formations. Don't forget to pick up a trail leaflet from the Information Centre at Sedbergh.
Map:	OS Outdoor Leisure 2 Yorkshire Dales, western area

The Walk

From the car park take the narrow lane, signposted Sedgwick Trail, which drops steadily downhill to cross Danny Bridge over the Clough River. Pause here to enjoy the boisterous stream and then climb the slope beyond. Follow the narrow road as it bears right and continue on the high-level way. It is edged with scattered ash and hawthorn. To your left the lonely slopes of Baugh Fell steadily rise towards Knoutberry Haw, and across the river valley Rise Hill towers forbiddingly.

At the sign for Hole House Farm, where the road branches, take the

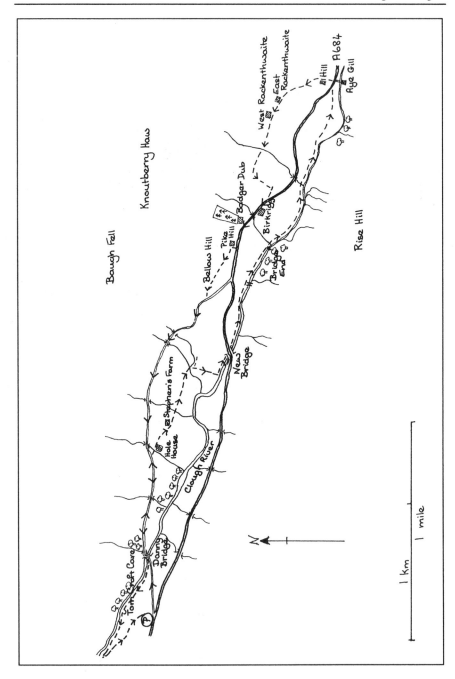

Bank barn

right fork, signposted New Bridge. Go on to pass between the buildings and through the gate ahead. Stride on to the next gate and then aim for an arrowed gate to the right of Stephen's Farm. Saunter ahead to the next gate. A good grassy trod continues and then comes beside a wall on your right. Over this is a pleasing glimpse of the Clough.

Pass through a gap stile and go on to a gated stile to the left of the topmost ash tree. The next stile lies to the left of a rather fine bank barn. Bear right on a track to a waymarked gate. Beyond, walk ahead towards the side of the river. Here herons often feed. At the river bank, turn left and continue to steps that lead up to New Bridge, which carries the A684. Cross the A-road with care, and continue on the glorious footpath, in the direction of Aye Gill, remaining on the same bank of the Clough.

Look for the gap stile, where you are asked to keep in single file over the pasture ahead and to keep all dogs on leads. Pass through a gate and, beyond, turn right to walk a reinforced track, with the river still to your right. Do not cross the bridge at Bridge End, but look for the hidden stile down on your left. Across on the other bank stands a forlorn Methodist chapel which was built in 1863 and now, sadly, is used as a barn for storing hay.

Stroll on along the stiled path beside the beck, where tree creepers

Heron

search for insects. Pass through stiles on the river side of an area used for abandoned vehicles. Go past two small bridges to climb a sturdy stile. Beyond the next gate, keep to the left of the fence with the river still to your right. Go through two more gated stiles and then strike diagonally left across a large pasture to a stile onto the A684.

Stride right for 50 metres and then cross the road to take a signposted left turn to Birkrigg. Follow the grassy path through a hedged and walled way. Climb the slope left and go on to pass through a gate into a farmyard. Walk ahead to pass through another gate (look for the 'FP's painted in white). Turn left to walk behind the farmhouse and then strike away from it through a gap in a wall. Go on to a gate in the wall on your left. Continue on the same diagonal through stiles to come to a gate to a walled track at East Rackenthwaite. Walk left along the track, passing in front of the farmhouse, which has a fine corbelled chimney. Beyond the gate at the end of the track, go right to pass through another.

Continue on in the same general direction to climb a stile up against the wall of West Rackenthwaite farmhouse. Walk in front of the dwelling, bear left to pass the outbuildings on the right and then, immediately, stroll right across the pasture to a stile in the wall. As you go on under the slopes of Knoutberry Haw, your path is bisected by innumerable streams that tumble down its slopes, all of them crossed by a step.

Saunter the stiled way to a gate before a barn. Walk a track to its left and follow it as it swings left to pass through a large gate to join a metalled track. At the three-armed signpost, turn right to walk beside a wall to a rickety stile to the A684, with Birkrigg on the opposite side.

Walk right, with extreme care, for a quarter-of-a-mile along the A-road, where the verge provides very little refuge. Pass two dwellings, Badger Dub and Pike Hill and beyond the latter turn right into a wide, reinforced track, signposted Bellow Hill. After a few metres, take the gate on the left and cross the pasture to a stile in the wall. Step over the stream and head on, bearing right, towards a wall. Go on beside it, on your right, to a stile in the corner of two walls. Stride on, cross an access track and continue beside the wall to another stile at another wall junction – and deep in dense vegetation. Step across the verge to a narrow lane, where you turn right.

From now on the lane, gated regularly, leads you delectably back to Danny Bridge. Beyond, turn right to walk the geological trail along the bank of the Clough River. Each point of interest is marked with a numbered post and here you should make full use of your leaflet.

At point 1 you can see a fine exposure of Great Scar limestone, formed about 330 million years ago. The long, slanting (60 degrees) cracks are known as bedding planes. At point 2 look down on the rocks to see white marks that are fossilised shellfish known as brachiopods.

At point 3 you pass deep gullies. These remained after shale (mudrock which often separates beds of limestone) filled the gullies and was then eroded. At point 4 you might spot, on the rocks in front of you, a tiny patch of a black, shiny, coal-like substance known as chert. From post 5 look across the Clough to see some arched rocks. The upfold is called an anticline and downstream is a syncline – a down folding. The folding was caused by compression from other rocks.

Look for the steps that take you down to the riverside for point 6. Upstream you can see sandstone, which the leaflet explains reveals a change in conditions millions of years ago. Go on along the riverside to point 7, and Tom Croft Cave, where the limestone has been folded into a vertical position. Also look for the variety of mosses, ferns and liverworts luxuriating on the moist, shady rocks of the cave entrance.

Leave the riverside and climb with care up the steepish slope. Suddenly the gorge ends, the riverbed widens and the water is shallower and placid. Ahead the narrow path is slashed by a narrow, shallow gully descending to the Clough. This is the Dent Fault and the leaflet tells you that this is where the Dales meet the Lake District. Before you cross the gully, the rocks you are standing on are 100 million years younger than those on the other side.

Descend the steps to a stile over a fence at the side of the river. Walk right (upstream) to come to point 9. Here you are on the Dales side of the Dent Fault, where the limestone has been broken into tiny fragments, known as breccia. Return to the stile but do not cross. Walk on to point 10 where you can see rocks known as Brathay Flags. These were laid down 425 million years ago. Close by is a huge rock face of red pebbles embedded in a rock matrix. This is known as conglomerate.

It may be possible to walk on to point 11 and 12, but if the river is high, return to the stile and climb up inside the fence. Follow it round to a stile, beyond which a small path descends to the riverside. Here in a delightful, sheltered hollow you can see more Brathay Flags and conglomerate.

Return to the stile above points 11 and 12 and walk back along the fence. Where the gorge begins, look for a grassy trod that becomes clearer as it crosses the common, returning you to the car park. Here you can often see fell ponies grazing – you are asked not to feed them.

The trail was opened in 1985 to commemorate the bicentenary of Adam Sedgwick, Professor of Geology at Cambridge. It was developed by the Yorkshire Dales National Park, English Nature and the Yorkshire Dales Society. Sedgwick was born in Dent and attended Dent and Sedbergh schools.

Walk 3: Rawthey Bridge – Uldale

Rawthey Bridge – Needlehouse Bridge – Rawthey Gill
Quarry – Slate Gill – Uldale Force – Needlehouse –
Wraygreen – Rawthey Bridge

Start/finish: A very large lay-by on the A683 immediately before Rawthey Bridge on the south-west side, 6 miles from Sedbergh (GR 713973).

Type of walk: When you set off on this 4½ mile walk from the severe surrounds of Rawthey Bridge, the unexpected tree-lined valley through which rushes the River Rawthey comes as a delightful surprise. The waterfalls are magnificent and the colours of the trees in autumn are breath-taking. A narrow white-knuckle path takes you close to the top fall, Uldale Force, but walking this is not to be recommended for families with children, for not-quite-so-young fell walkers or for those with no head for heights. Each time the writer has walked it she decided never again, but it is easy to find yourself on the path, with a long perpendicular drop on one side, before you realise where you are, lured on by the magnificent force ahead. Be warned.

Map: OS Outdoor Leisure 19 Howgill Fells and Upper Eden Valley

The Walk

Cross the road from the parking area. Follow the signpost directions for the bridleway to Uldale and Bluecaster Side. Pass through the gate and walk on to follow the reinforced track as it swings right, passing through a marshy area before a dry way is attained. Climb the grassy trod until you reach the brow. Go on over another marshy

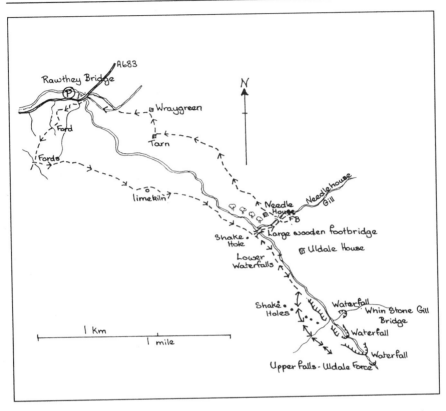

area (almost a ford) and then leave the green way – the old road that goes on along the side of Bluecaster – to turn sharp left for Uldale.

Follow the clear track, which regularly crosses small marshy areas. They are marked 'ford' on the OS map and can be negotiated by making use of convenient stones and rushes. As you go, look down on the lively Rawthey dancing between its tree-lined banks and over its rocky bed. Look for the ruined limekiln on the right of the path. In spring and summer listen for the bubbling calls of curlews and the sweet songs of meadow pipits. Press on along the good track as it takes you gently downhill into mid-Uldale and to a sturdy wooden bridge over the Rawthey.

Stand on this excellent viewing platform for the best sight of the Lower Falls as the Rawthey descends in elegant cascades, foaming white-topped as it rushes on its way. It then rages through a deep,

tree-shadowed can-
yon, its sides bright
with emerald green
moss and ferns.

Do not cross the
bridge but continue
along the overgrown
rough track, an old
quarry road, with the
cascades to your left.
Pause here to look for
dipppers – white-bib-
bed, rotund, black
birds that frequent the
shallows, running in and out of the water after aquatic insects. Often
one will stand on a boulder, mid-stream, and bob up and down.

Curlew

Go on, with the opposite bank of the river clad with glorious
mixed woodland. Towards the end of the trees, look down on
another splendid fall that descends over stepped rocks in a cloud of
spray beneath birch, hazel, scots pine and holly. Here look up the
slope on your right to see an indistinct grassy track sloping upwards.
Scramble up to join this track, which soon ceases and then, shortly,
reappears as a narrow path across the higher slopes.

Look left across the Rawthey to see the dramatic fall that descends
through a tree-lined ravine over stepped rocks. This is Whin Stone
Gill. Stroll on to the edge of Slate Gill and cross it above the highest
rowan. Look ahead for your first glorious glimpse of Uldale Force,
where the Rawthey drops in long white tresses for twenty feet or
more into a foaming pool.

This may be the point of your return. Or you may wish to go on
the continuing narrow path. On your way you pass, far down,
another pleasing waterfall. By staying on this path you avoid the
difficult narrow traverse lower down the steep slopes.

Return along the narrow trod, cross Slate Gill and look back for
another great view of the Upper Falls. Go on the narrow path and
then the indistinct grassy track that leads down to come beside the

fall at the edge of the plantation of mixed woodland. Turn left and continue along the lovely way to cross the wooden bridge.

Uldale – Lower fall

Stride the wide track below lofty beech. Just beyond the gate look for the easy-to-miss step stile in the remnant of wall on your left. Beyond, stride a shelf-like path, below beech, and above the beck in Needlehouse Gill. Follow the path down to cross a footbridge. Go on to keep to the right of the first house. Bear left behind it and then right to pass in front of another house. Look for the round chimneys and the bell on the barn.

Take the right of two gates and saunter on for fifty metres. Then strike diagonally right, over the pasture. From here you can see Cautley Spout, and the limekiln passed on your outward route. Pass through the gate and go on, with mixed woodland to your right and a fir plantation ahead. Walk on to cross a grassy bridge into the next pasture, with New House ahead and a magnificent view of the Howgills beyond.

Keep to the left of the fine dwelling, pass through a gate behind the house and go on along a walled track. At its end, swing left, take the gate on the right and continue on through the middle of the pasture to a gap stile in the wall ahead. Beyond, walk ahead to pass through the gate in the left corner. Proceed with the wall to the left and then walk the gated, cobbled way at Tarn Farm. Go on, bearing slightly right to a gap stile at the side of a gate. Head on to the left of Wraygreen Farm. Go through the gate and turn left to walk beside the wall on the left. Pass through the gate, turn right and walk to the gate to the road. Turn left to rejoin your car.

Walk 4: Rawthey Bridge – Stennerskeugh and Fell End Clouds

Rawthey Bridge – Murthwaite – Fell End – The Street – Clouds – Stennerskeugh Clouds – Fell End Clouds – The Street – Rawthey Bridge

Start/finish: A very large lay-by south-west of Rawthey Bridge on the A683. The A-road links Sedbergh with Kirkby Stephen and the parking area lies 6 miles from Sedbergh (GR 713979).

Type of walk: A quiet 7½-miler. It starts with a steepish field climb to a farm tucked under Wandale Hill. It continues by a reinforced lane to Fell End. Another steadily climbing track takes you up to The Street, a virtually traffic-free highway, once a Roman road. After a quick 'scoot' along the A-road you climb Clouds Lane, a secluded track that takes you onto Clouds, the vast magical limestone skirts of Wild Boar Fell. The return route is back along The Street.

Map: OS Outdoor Leisure 19 Howgill Fells and Upper Eden Valley

The Walk

Walk on from the parking area to cross the high, wide Rawthey Bridge. Pass an old milestone that says you are 8 miles from Kirkby Stephen. Go on for 365 metres. Ignore the tractor bridge on the left to take, almost immediately, the footbridge beyond.

Climb straight up the steep fellside to a stile in the hedge. Beyond, go on up to the fence ahead, passing through a gate in the left corner. Keep watch for roe deer that are sometimes seen grazing here. Stroll on, bearing slightly right to a gap stile in the wall ahead, keeping

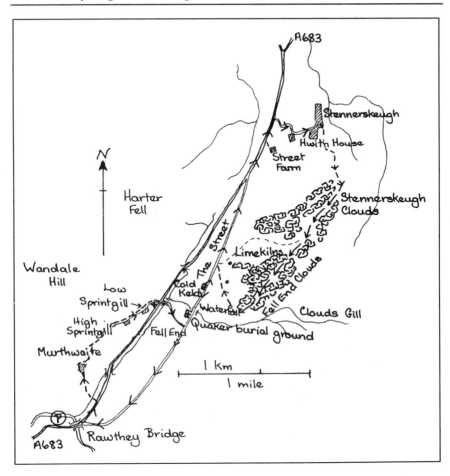

left of a stretch of wall that stands forlorn. Walk on towards the farm at Murthwaite. Pass through the gate to the left of the farmhouse, proceed ahead and follow the track as it swings right behind the dwelling. Go on along the access track to a gate to a lane.

Beyond, take the right fork. Stroll the reinforced track as it steadily descends. Pass High Sprintgill and then Low Sprintgill. Look for its bank barn with an arched passage way below its ramp. Opposite is an ornately housed drinking trough. Continue to the A683 and look right to see the tiny Wesleyan Methodist Chapel, finely maintained and with a datestone for 1861.

Cross the road and walk ahead along a wide track. Use the footbridge over the beck and stride a narrow, railed way above the hurrying stream. Ascend steadily to join the old road, believed to be Roman and known as The Street. It has been superseded by the A-road that runs along the valley bottom and is a quiet, airy highway from where there are delightful views.

Pass the old Quaker burial ground and just beyond, on the opposite side of the road, is a pleasing waterfall, where a stream rages over great plates of limestone. Press on to pass Cold Keld on the left. And then on the right Fell End Clouds and its several cairns come into view – 'clouds' meaning, aptly, a mass of stones.

Fell End Clouds – limestone pavement

Look right, on the lower slopes, to see a limekiln and then further on, along an unfenced part of the road, two more. Note this point because this is where you descend from the Clouds on your return. Pass a quarry on the right and then walk on to join the A-road, which is fortunately edged with wide grassy verges. On the far side of the road, a few stones are all that remain of a Quaker meeting house.

Stroll on to pass Street Farm, where a limekiln stands close to the road. Take the signposted right turn for Street and Stennerskeugh. Follow it as it swings left. Beside on your right are a high wall and tall trees. Among these is a castellated building, a remnant of Hwith House, demolished in 1927. It was once a fine house built in 1868 by John Hewetson, who gave it its strange name, composed of the initials of his five sons.

Take the first turning on the right, following the wall round, to walk Clouds Lane, a rough, walled track. Pass through a gate on to rolling moorland, with distant views of the Pennines. Follow the waymark directing you right to climb a faint track, with a wall to the right. As the wall turns away right, continue on and then bear right to walk a grassy terrace, with limestone walls stretching upwards to your left and clints and grykes descending to your right.

Dawdle along the grassy trods through this glorious limestone wonderland of Stennerskeugh Clouds. Ahead is a grand view of the Howgills. Cross Dale Slack, a fine grassy track used by lead miners on their way to workings higher up the fell. Beyond, continue on, keeping on more trods well above a magnificent sea of limestone. After you have passed all the cairns, seen earlier from the old road, go on to pick up another track to descend the slopes, keeping well to the left of the two limekilns also seen earlier.

Join The Street and walk left. Continue past the farms of Elm Pot, Ash Pot, Streetside and Foggy Gill, with Wild Boar Fell showing its less dramatic side to your left. Opposite the last farm stands the old Fell Side school, closed in 1946. In front of the building grows a sturdy sycamore tree, planted for the accession of Edward VIII. Stride on to cross Rawthey Bridge and to rejoin your car.

Roe Deer

Walk 5: Wild Boar Fell

Cotegill Bridge´– Near Cote Gill – Aisgill Moor – The Band
– Yoadcomb Scar – The Nab – Wild Boar Fell summit – The
Nab – White Walls – High Dolphinsty – Angerholme Wold –
Aisgill Farm – Cotegill Bridge

Start/finish:	A lay-by on the B6259, the road through Maller-stang. It lies on the south side of Cotegill Bridge, which crosses the Settle and Carlisle railway line (GR 774969).
Type of walk:	This 6½ mile walk is for strong walkers who can pick the easiest way over damp peaty Aisgill Moor. For those who have negotiated the climb down and then up, to cross Ais Gill, and then continued up to the ridge, a great reward follows. The way along the ridge is superb, with stunning views and easy walking. The return over Angerholme is pleasing and not such hard walking, though it too can be wet in parts. You may prefer to use this route for your approach, and return from Wild Boar Fell. There are no waymarks on this walk.
Map:	OS Outdoor Leisure 19 Howgill Fells and Upper Eden Valley

The Walk

Before you set off, look for the five bridges close to the lay-by, reminding you of the enormous amount of work required to construct the railway through Mallerstang. Look opposite to see the pretty waterfall tumbling down rocky ledges into an old quarry.

Go through the gate between the quarry and the railway bridge, on the other side of the road from the parking area. Follow the tractor route uphill, with Near Cote Gill to your left. As you climb to the

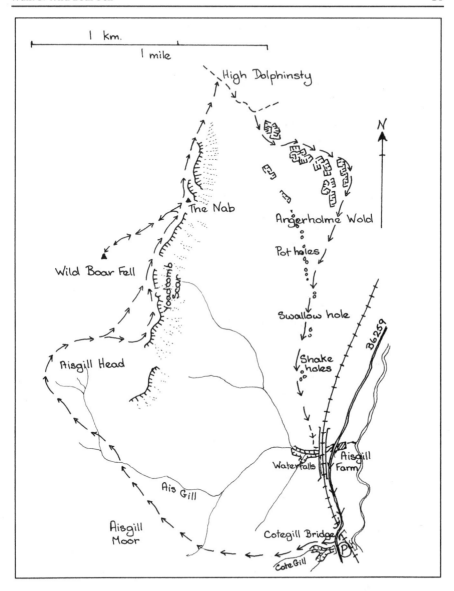

first small hill and the beck veers left, begin to bear more to the right, avoiding wet areas and peat hags.

Cross Low Soursike, choosing the easiest way, and continue across the wet moorland to come to the side of the much deeper gill through which flows Ais Beck. Again choose the easiest place to drop down to the hurrying stream and then climb up the steepish slope on the other side.

Continue on up – the way much drier now – to come to the extensive flattish top of Wild Boar Fell. Here stride ahead over the rough moorland, where strangely contorted summit boulders are scattered sparsely; millstones were cut from these. Or, with care, stroll the escarpment, from where there are tremendous views into the valley below and across to Mallerstang Edge.

At Yoadcombe Scar 2323ft (708m) there are a dozen or more well constructed cairns and two rough shelters.

Cairns on Yoadcombe Scar

Climb the small ladderstile over the fence and continue along dramatic Blackbed Scar to The Nab, 2303ft (702m). On its small mound it has a cairn. This is the shapely part of Wild Boar often spotted on other walks in this book. From it, the view is a delight. To the west you can see the white stones of Stennerskeugh Clouds visited on walk 4. Then peer beyond the Clouds to see Cautley Spout (walk 11) nestling among the Howgills. Looking down on them from this wild spot they seem like fairy hills with bright green, grassy slopes.

From The Nab follow the cairned path away from the edge in a south-westerly direction towards a pile of stone. This is the summit of Wild Boar, 2323ft (708m), where the trig point stands in a roughly built wind shelter. There is no view to speak of but on this high, bleak plateau it is not difficult to believe that, as tradition has it, the last wild boar in England was shot here. (The summit could have been reached by walking ahead from the ladderstile on Yoadcombe Scar and then continuing to The Nab, but then the fine escarpment walk would have been missed.)

Return to The Nab and, after enjoying the view, begin your descent of the north ridge. Pause half-way to look at the change of rocks. From this high point you can see where the limestone emerges from the overlying gritstone and shale, and where rough mat grass changes to sweet turf.

Descend to a wall corner, High Dolphinsty on the OS map, and turn right to join a delightful terrace-like path descending rapidly towards the right. As it ends in more rough grass, stride slightly left towards limestone pavement and a wall. Continue on, with the wall to your left, until it slopes away left. Here swing right and head towards a large cairn with, rather unexpectedly, a television aerial beside it.

Go on right to come beside another wall on your left. Keep parallel with this for just over a mile. As you go you pass more limestone pavement and small, hidden, grassy gills, each with its own dancing beck. You also pass several swallow holes and potholes. Take great care if you approach the latter as all are unfenced and several are very dangerous. The entrances of some are adorned with delightful fern gardens.

Follow the wall as it turns down left to come to the side of the railway line and walk on along the track to the fine viaduct by Aisgill Farm. Pause here to view the glorious waterfall on Ais Gill Beck. Pass under the viaduct and follow the track to the road. Turn right and walk back along the B6259 to rejoin your car.

Walk 6: Hell Gill – Outhgill, Mallerstang

Cotegill Bridge – Aisgill Moor Cottages – Hellgill – The
Highway – Thrang Bridge – Outhgill – Sycamore Tree Farm
– Deepgill – Hazelgill Farm – Cooper Hill – Ing Heads –
Hanging Lund – Aisgill Farm – Cotegill Bridge

Start/finish:	A lay-by on the B6259, the road through Maller-stang. It lies on the south side of Cotegill Bridge which crosses the Settle and Carlisle railway line (GR 774969) (see walk 5).
Type of walk:	This splendid 7-miler takes you first high above the glorious Mallerstang Valley, following the way taken by the 17th century Lady Ann Clifford. After a dry spell you can swing along the wide track, with magic views ahead, all the way to the young River Eden. After wet weather you will have to pick your way. A footpath takes you beside the river – pleasingly so – to visit St Mary's Church at the hamlet of Outhgill. The return presents more of a challenge, with map-reading required to help you along tracks and paths between farms where there are few waymarks to help. All farm tracks can be muddy after rain. As you explore this quiet valley you are overlooked, to the west, by imposing Wild Boar Fell (walk 5) and, to the east, by magnificent Mallerstang Edge.
Map:	OS Outdoor Leisure 19 The Howgills and the Eden Valley

The Walk

From the lay-by walk south along the B-road, with the railway to
your left and Swarth Fell to your right. Continue until you reach
Aisgill Moor Cottages, formerly railway cottages. Beyond the last

building, Aisgill Crafts and Tearooms, take, on the left, the signposted track for Hellgill. Cross the bridge over the railway and follow the track left.

Just before it swings right, take a short grassy path, left, to view the magnificent Hellgill Force. Here the Hellgill Beck leaps over 60ft into a plunge pool and becomes the infant River Eden. In summer its rocky amphitheatre is lined with flowers and the rowans, sheltering in the gill, are heavily laden with creamy blossoms.

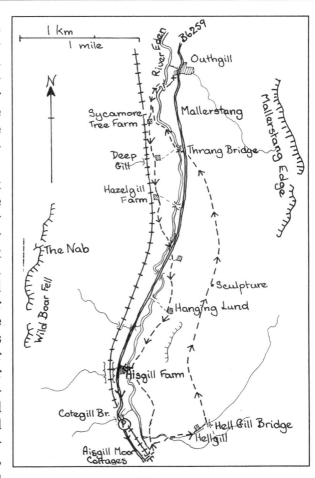

Return to the track. Do not cross the ford but follow the track as it swings right and continues on to cross a tractor bridge over the Hellgill Beck. Stride on through pastures, aglow with kingcups in June. From them come the calls of curlews. Pass to the right of Hellgill Farm and go on to the gated Hell Gill Bridge. Stand on the bridge and, if the season is not too advanced, peer over the parapet into the fearsome canyon below. Legend has it that Dick Turpin leapt across it, escaping from Yorkshire into the old Westmorland, to avoid capture, but his companion's horse baulked at the lip of the ravine and threw his rider over its head, into the boiling cauldron far below. His body was found downstream several days later.

Do not cross the bridge, but turn left to walk The Highway, a wide grassy way with the fell wall to the left. Mary Queen of Scots travelled along this track on her way to imprisonment in Castle Bolton. A century later Lady Anne Clifford travelled the same route in her horse litter to inspect the restoration done on her castle at Pendragon. She also renovated her other castles at Skipton, Brougham, Appleby and Brough. A devout Christian, she also built or restored churches and almshouses.

Stride the glorious track for a mile, where in spring you might see green plovers and red-shanks. Then the wall turns away left and here, on the track, stands an enormous sculpture, two huge slabs of limestone embedded in another. The slabs have curving sides and face each other, the curves representing the banks of the River Eden, winding through Mallerstang.

Sculpture: 'Water Cut' by Mary Bourne

It is from this point that the lovely valley is best seen, wedged between the two great fells. You can see the river, the railway and the road sharing the valley bottom. Pleasing walls stretch up the slopes and form enclosures, many with their own stone barn. Clumps of trees stand about the farmsteads, dotted in and just above the valley bottom.

Beyond the sculpture, the track begins its descent for a mile-and-a-half over the rough fell. It crosses several small fords and its surface becomes rutted. This is the territory of skylarks, and in summer they fill the air with their lovely trills.

The track brings you to the side of the B-road. Turn right and, after a few steps, cross the road to take the track on the left, signposted Deepgill. Follow the track as it winds left, and then right over the top of a small limekiln, to come to Thrang Bridge, a packhorse bridge over the River Eden. Here you will be tempted to take your first break.

Beyond the bridge, turn right to walk beside the alder and elm-edged chuckling stream. Climb the stile over the wall and continue on beside the river. Ignore the footbridge over the river and stroll on to pass through a gate. Follow the wooded riverside track to come to the stock sheds of Sycamore Tree Farm.

Look for the small footpath sign, directing you left, between the buildings. Ignore the gate on your left (to be taken on your return route) and follow the metalled way as it swings right, for 45 metres. Take the narrow path on the left, which cuts straight across a meadow to a fine gap stile in the wall. Beyond, walk ahead to come beside the Eden, still on your right, and follow the clear path through the trees to cross a rough tractor bridge over the lovely river.

Immediately beyond, climb a stile on your left, its posts painted a bright red. Stroll the glorious path across two hay meadows to the gate to Outhwaite church. Pause here to look at the sturdy little building in its idyllic setting. Its bell is believed to be 13th-century and one of the oldest in the diocese, but where it came from, and under what circumstances is not recorded.

As you enter the door, look at the plaque above it. It describes how Lady Anne Clifford had the church restored in 1663 after it had 'layne ruinous and decayed'. Records show that a church had existed in 1535 but it is believed that an earlier church had been built in 1311 by another redoubtable lady – Lady Idonea de Vetaripont who had lived at Pendragon Castle. The plaque, which replaced the original in 1909, ends with a reference to chapter 58, Verse 12, of Isaiah: 'They that shall be of Thee shall build the old waste places.'

Leave the church by the same gate and return over the meadows to climb the red-topped stile. Beyond the tractor bridge, turn left to walk beside the Eden, where you might see dippers and sandpipers. When the trees cease, walk right across a meadow, away from the river, to the gap stile in the wall. Continue to the gate, now on your right, ignored on your outward route.

Sandpiper

Go through and climb the access track, and continue where it bends sharply left, to walk towards the farmhouse of Sycamore Tree Farm. From here you can see much of the valley and the area where you walked The Highway. High up on the moor stands the sculpture. Follow the track behind the farmhouse, with the Settle and Carlisle railway up on your right.

From now on you should practise your map reading skills. Stride the clear way. Beyond a ruined barn it becomes less clear but carry on towards another barn and pass to the right of it. Follow the now clearer track over Cowstead Gill and go on across the pasture ahead, keeping parallel with the railway high on your right.

Cross the next stile and stroll on to pass behind Deepgill Farm, once a Quaker meeting place. Cross a small bridge over Deep Gill and keep beside the wall on your left. Saunter ahead to cross three stiled pastures to pass behind Hazelgill Farm.

Just beyond the buildings, ignore the track which leads up right to pass under the railway. Go through a gate on the left and then continue on in the same general direction, shortly to walk with the wall again to your left. Pass through another stiled pasture, still with the wall to the left. Continue on to walk to the right of a stone barn. Go on the stiled way over a pasture below Hall Hill and through a gated stile. Walk on to a gap stile. Beyond, bear left across the pasture towards a barn, close beside the River Eden, which you cross by a tractor bridge to join the road.

Cross the road, with care, and take the signposted gap stile. Cross the pasture corner, right, to another gap stile onto the access track to Cooper Hill Farm. (If the last stile is blocked, to prevent lambs getting through, use the access track.) Follow the access track uphill, with a glorious haymeadow to the right. Just before the first barn (black) turn right to pass through a difficult gate.

Stride ahead to a narrow gap stile into the front garden of Ing Heads (1688). Leave the garden by the signposted gate on your right. Immediately swing left and walk through newly planted trees to a stile beside a gate in the wall ahead. Head across the pasture (do not climb left towards a barn), in the direction of a white farmhouse, to take the next stile in the wall, beside a telegraph pole. Stride on towards another, with a large yellow disc above it.

Go ahead towards the front of the immaculate Hanging Lund dwelling (the white farmhouse is immediately behind it). Just before the house, look left to see the spectacular waterfall hurtling down the hillside.

Follow the well-waymarked, gated route to pass in front of the dwelling. Walk a plank over a stream and stroll ahead. In the next pasture stands a barn with a gap stile in the wall close to it. Ignore this and pass through a wall gap to the right of the stile to join a causeway path that keeps beside the wall on your left. Go on over the rough pasture to climb the high stile in the wall corner and walk on to pass through the wall gap ahead. Continue through the next gap and walk ahead to the next gap stile. Ignore the bridge to the right and walk ahead to a difficult-to-locate step stile in the wall ahead.

Beyond the stile, walk beside a wall on your right, over which you can see the River Eden. Remain with the wall to walk to the bridge over the river. Cross and continue to Aisgill Farm, where you bear right to pass through two gates to join the road.

Turn left and walk the B-road uphill for a quarter of a mile to rejoin your car, beyond Cotegill Bridge.

Walk 7: Nateby – Pendragon and Lammerside Castle

Nateby – Thringill – Southwaite – Pendragon – Birkett
Common – Lammerside Castle – Wharton Hall – Nateby

Start/finish:	Nateby lies one and a half miles from Kirkby Stephen. Leave your car in one of two lay-bys, either at the northern or southern edge of the village on the B6259 (GR of village green 775068).
Type of walk:	This is a delightful seven-miler that goes through pastures, crosses the lower slopes of Great Bell, views Pendragon Castle, keeps company with the River Eden to Lammerside Castle, passes in front of the glorious Wharton Hall and then treads between outcrops of brockram to return to Nateby.
Map:	OS Outdoor Leisure 19 Howgill Fells and Upper Eden Valley

The Walk

The small village of Nateby snuggles round a tiny green. It is a friendly place. It has a Methodist church and a petrol station, with a useful shop attached. Opposite is the welcoming Black Bull Inn, with a yellow AA sign on its wall recording that it is 267 miles to London.

Leave the village by the B6270, in the direction of Swaledale. The road turns east opposite the inn. Walk ahead to take a footpath on the right, signposted Bells. Before you walk the shady track, look to the other side of the road to see picturesque Wellhead Cottage, with its two porches.

The quiet, walled way steadily ascends. After passing through two gates, walk ahead, continuing over a stone stepped stile in the boundary wall. Before you is a first dramatic view of Wild Boar Fell,

with bleak, riven Mallerstang Edge to your left. Go on to take a gate
on your right, 90 metres before the next cross wall. This gives access
to the B6259.

Turn left and after 45 metres take the signposted gate on the left.
Strike diagonally across the pasture to the far corner to pass through
a gate with a white-topped post beside it. Walk on, with the wall to

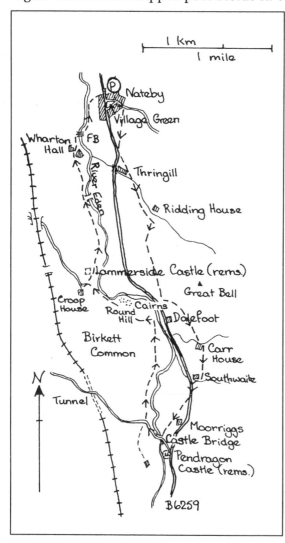

your right, towards a
similar post. Where
the wall turns away,
stroll on to come be-
side another wall on
the right. Look for the
third post, partially
obscured by a syca-
more, marking a stone
stile over the wall.
(Take care on this
stile, it is not easy for
short-legged walkers.)

Beyond, cross the
bed of Thringill Beck
and go on in the same
general direction,
again with a wall to
your right. Begin to
climb gently to pass
through a gate, with
the beck to your left.
Walk on, keeping to
the left of a derelict
wall, in the direction
of forlorn Ridding
House. Pass through
the gate onto the
slopes of Great Bell.
Stride the grassy trod
ahead for a short dis-

tance and then take another that bears off right. Enjoy the glorious view of the Howgills to the right of Wild Boar Fell. In the same direction you might glimpse traffic on the Carlistle and Settle railway, passing through heather slopes, colourful in season.

Continue on the same contour, below Great Bell and well above the River Eden. Look across the river to low Round Hill, its cairns (burial mounds) clearly seen as raised oblong shapes.

Head across the lovely slopes, aiming for the left of the fell wall above Dalefoot Farm. Pass below scattered forest trees to a stile. Beyond, join a good track and pass below more trees and follow the way as it winds downhill, under alder, to pass in front of ruined Carr House. Go through the gap stile and walk on directly ahead to a step stile, where two walls join.

Once over, step across the small stream and stride on. Before the next deepish gill, look for the step stile, over the wall, on your right, and follow the path towards two dwellings at Southwaite. A gate on your left gives access to a track. Follow it and

heather

continue where it turns right to rejoin the B6259. Turn left and walk on for 185 metres to the signposted footpath on the right.

Pass through the gate and strike left across the pasture to a stone step stile in a 2 metre stretch of wall set in the boundary fence. Go ahead, with Mooriggs Farm to the left, to the far right corner. Ahead you can see Pendragon Castle. Pass through the gate and take another immediately right. Walk left, with the fence to your left, and continue to take a stile over it. Head for the signposted stile to the left of Castle Bridge (over the River Eden).

Pendragon Castle

To see the castle turn left and walk a short way along the lane. There is a good view, over the wall, of the moated ruin, with Wild Boar Fell towering above. Tradition says that the castle is named after its builder, Uther Pendragon, the father of King Arthur. Its 12th-century owner was Hugh de Morville, who was involved in the murder of Thomas a Becket. In the early 14th century it was burnt down by marauding Scots, and later rebuilt by Richard de Clifford, only to be burnt down again. By 1661, his famous descendant and restorer of the family's castles, Lady Ann Clifford, was able to sleep in it, and in 1663 she and her family spent Christmas here.

Return to cross the bridge over the Eden and follow the narrow lane uphill and where it swings right. Cross the cattle grid and turn right to take the bridleway for Wharton, with Birkett Common to the left and the Eden below on your right. A tunnel through the Common carries the railway. Enjoy the pleasing views from the glorious grassy track. Pass a limekiln and continue to Birkett Bottom where, at the division of tracks, you turn left to walk to the south-west of Round Hill, seen earlier from across the valley.

Go through the gate on the track and as you near Croop House take the next gate, immediately on your right. Walk ahead to the ruin of Lammerside Castle, a fortified building, which commands a pleasing view of the vale. Notice the fine vaulted roof of its lowest chamber. Pass through the gate beyond and head for the next one in the far right corner of the fence. Stroll on, slightly climbing, to pass through a wooden gate, and take the next one, uphill again.

With the fence, much tree planting and the river to your right, go on along the large pasture to pass through a double-sized farm gate to a track. Turn right and walk on. This concreted track passes in front of Wharton Hall. (As this book went to press, there was a possibility that this track might be diverted, but if so it would be well signposted.)

The hall, erected in the 14th century, has an impressive gate-house, constructed in 1559 by one of the all-powerful Whartons. In 1728 the family forfeited the estate and it fell into ruins. Today, though not open to the public, it has been restored to considerable magnificence by the present owners.

Continue ahead along the track to two signposts. Climb the stile on your right and drop down the pasture to a wooden tractor bridge over the Eden. Beyond, turn left and follow the river bank to pass through a gate. Continue on the well-waymarked, steadily climbing path to pass outcroppings of pink conglomerate, brockram, where rock fragments are embedded by nature in a reddish matrix. Continue on a gated track to return to the village. Turn right to return to the village green.

Walk 8: Kirkby Stephen – Nateby

Kirkby Stephen – Frank's Bridge – Nateby – Wharton Hall –
Halfpenny House – Croglam Castle (earthwork) – Kirkby
Stephen

Start/finish:	Free car park by Kirkby Stephen School, north-west end of the town.(GR 774088)
Type of walk:	This pleasant 4½ mile walk starts with a visit to the impressive parish church, set back in its own quiet close. It continues to Frank's Bridge, crosses the River Eden and then continues beside the lovely river. A delightful bridleway takes you to the small village of Nateby. Then it's on again across the meadows, and over the Eden once more, with just a fleeting glimpse of Wharton Hall. Tracks and paths, eventually leading to the foot of ancient earthworks, are followed by a final glorious footpath all the way from Greenriggs Farm back to the town.
Map:	OS Outdoor Leisure 19 Howgill Fells and Upper Eden Valley

The Walk

From the car park take the signposted 'Footpath to the town centre'. On reaching a road, cross and walk the ginnel ahead, leading to the main street and the market place which, if it's Monday, will be full of lively stalls.

Close by are the Cloisters, built in 1810 to provide shelter for people attending the market or church. On the wall a board gives the market rules and other panels record much interesting history of the old market town.

Pass through the fine cloisters into the close in front of St

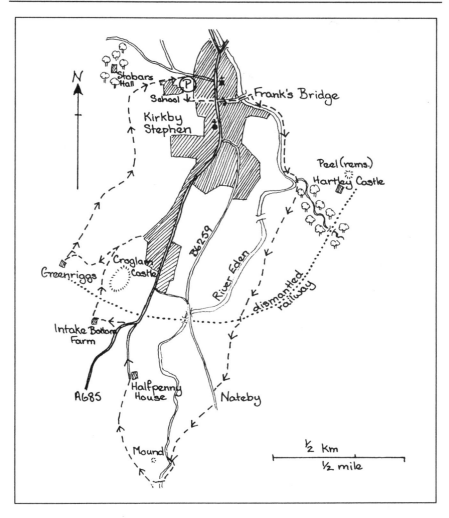

Stephen's Church. This is often known as the cathedral of the dale because of its great length. To go inside use the door on the side. Wander around the lovely interior. Look for the Loki stone, a 10th-century Anglo-Danish cross shaft carved into the bearded figure of a chained devil, representing the old Norse god Loki.

Don't miss the Wharton Chapel on the north side of the chancel. It contains a tomb with effigies of Thomas, first Lord of Wharton, with his first wife on one side and his second on the other. Walk 7 took you past Wharton Hall, and on this one you can see it through the trees.

Visit the Hartley chapel to see the tomb of Sir Richard de Musgrave, who died in 1464. Tradition has it that he killed the last boar on Wild Boar Fell (see walk 5). The tusk of a boar was found in his tomb during the 19th-century restoration of the chapel. It can be seen in a glass-topped showcase towards the back of the church. Leave the church by the cloisters and turn left to pass the toilets. Stroll on along a narrow street to follow a signpost directing you down steps to Frank's Bridge. Once over the River Eden, turn right to take the footpath for Nateby. It continues beside the hurrying river, where alders trail over the water and many ducks congregate.

Pass through a kissing gate and leave the well made path to walk right, continuing beside the river. High up on the hill, almost hidden by trees, is Hartley Farm, site of Hartley Castle. In the middle of the 14th century Hartley Castle passed into the hands of the Musgraves, which explains the burial of Sir Richard in the Hartley chapel.

Pass a fine bank barn on your left and then continue beside the river as it makes a swing to the left and becomes very deep. Here a collier was drowned, and ever since it has been known as Collier Dub.

Red Squirrel

Continue to a gated footbridge over Ladthwaite Beck, which joins the Eden here. Beyond the bridge, stride the lovely path through the trees of Podgill, where you might see red squirrels. Continue ahead along a fenced path, ignoring paths off right and left. Stroll on through the quiet countryside, following the path downhill to a stream and then as it climbs steadily uphill. In spring curlews call from pastures on both sides of the path.

Press on to cross a railway bridge over a dismantled railway (the same one on walk 24), and go on along the glorious hedged way. Just before the farm on the edge of Nateby, bear right, step across Broad Ing Sike and walk on to the B6259. Cross the road and walk left for a few steps to take a broad track going off on the right before the first house of the village.

Kirkby Stephen

Stride on the gated way beyond the houses of the village to open land where you can see large exposures of brochram, a conglomerate of bits of limestone in a matrix of sandstone. This is the stone used to build many of the houses in Kirkby Stephen. As you near a fenced area, descend with a fence to your left past more shallow cliffs of brochram to come to a kissing gate. Beyond continue beside the River Eden as it flows through this idyllic corner.

Cross the wide footbridge, observing the notice about the holes in the planking. Just beyond, look left to see Wharton Hall (see walk 7). Climb straight uphill to the two signposts, where you turn right to walk the concrete track in the direction of Halfpenny House. Look for two limekilns as you go.

Go over the cattle grid and walk the metalled road, which is edged with walls of brockram, to the side of the A685. Turn left and walk the grassy verge. Cross the A-road with care to take the track signposted Croglam Lane. Climb the waymarked sturdy stile, on the right, just before Intake Bottom farm. Stroll on and, ignoring the stile to the left, cross the gated bridge over the dismantled railway. Walk ahead, keeping above the gorse bushes, to wind right round the mound called Croglam Castle. Continue on to climb two stiles, the second signposted and to be found in the wall on your left. Beyond, turn left to walk the delightful lane leading towards Greenriggs Farm. Take the unmarked gate on the right 90 metres before the gate across the lane. Once through turn right to walk beside the hedge on your right.

From now on the delectable path leads to a gate and then a gap stile and on through quiet countryside. Turn right before a way-marked gate to take a stile into a walled track on your left. Where the track swings sharp right, go on through a waymarked stile to continue. Take the next stile beside the wall on the right. Ignore the stile into the school grounds and saunter on to a gate into a track, where you turn right. Away to the left is the crenellated Stobars Hall. Walk on to the road. Bear right and drop down to the car park, which is on the right.

Walk 9: Cross Keys – Wandale Hill

Cross Keys Inn – Backside Beck ford – Narthwaite –
Adamthwaite – Wandale Hill – Narthwaite – Backside Beck
ford – Cautley

Type of walk: Choose a fine day for this pleasing 5-miler. The views from the top of Wandale Hill, 1630ft (497m), are spectacular and the quiet unfrequented pastures a joy to walk. The ford over Backside Beck can be tiresome – or some say challenging – after heavy rain, so pick a dry spell.

Start/finish: A largish lay-by beyond Cross Keys Inn at Cautley (GR 698969), 4½ miles from Sedbergh on the A683, which continues to Kirkby Stephen.

Map: OS Outdoor Leisure 19 Howgill Fells and Upper Eden Valley

The Walk

Descend the steps from the parking area to cross the footbridge over the River Rawthey. From the bridge you can often see a dipper. Follow the path to a wide track, where you turn right and continue to climb gently. A pretty tree-lined gill lies to your right and through it hurries Backside Beck. Go on beside a wall on the right and then descend to the side of the beck, which you cross, either by boulder hopping, wading or removing your boots and paddling.

Climb the track ahead, which has a mixed conifer plantation to the left. Follow the track as it swings left towards the outbuildings of Narthwaite. Pass through a gate, and turn left to walk a track. Once beyond the next gate, continue ahead up a rough, grooved track. Go on through the right of two gates.

Stroll on the lovely way. Look right to see the tree-clad Uldale extending into the dour slopes of Baugh Fell. It is possible to pick

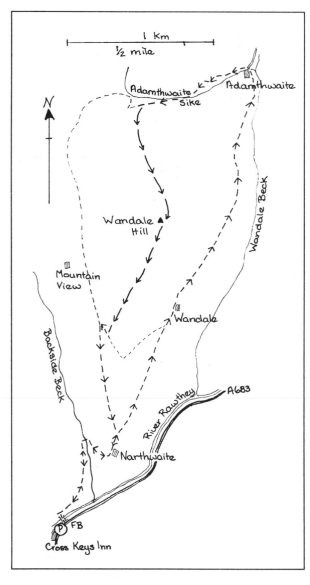

out the waterfall viewed on walk 3. From the track you can look down to see Rawthey Bridge. The continuing way is lined with straggly hawthorns.

And then the rounded top of Wandale Hill comes into view on your left. Pass the ruins of Wandale and go on through a gate. Beyond stretches the grand terrace-like way, which leads easily into the depths of the hills. Below, to the right, the beck is lined with deciduous trees and beyond stretch the slopes of Harter Fell (walk 28).

Go past more ruined buildings and under ash, the haunt of fieldfares in winter. At the division of the ways, keep to the right branch to walk a walled track to Adamthwaite farmhouse, which has a datestone inscribed 1684. The attractive dwelling stands in a tree-encircled hollow at the end of a narrow lane that runs south from Ravenstonedale.

Fieldfares

P a s s through the gate and cross a tractor bridge over the beck. Go on to pass through another gate to the road. Ignore this and walk the rough track, climbing left, with a wall to the left and the rolling fells to the right. Continue to pass through a gate and walk on. Step over a small beck and bear left along a faint green trod in the direction of a barn on your left. Do not take the gate beside it, but keep to the grassy trod that runs near to the wall on your left to come to a gate. Beyond, two streams unite. One is Adamthwaite Sike. Step across and follow the continuing narrow trod. Away to your right, beyond Grere Fell, towers Green Bell, visited on walk 29.

At the first small rise in the path, leave it, bear left and climb the slope, walking over mat grass, heather, square rush and sphagnum. Use the last two as indicators in avoiding wet areas. Continue to the top and wander around the broad, flat summit, which has a small pool but no cairn. Enjoy the spectacular view. Look east to see Fell End Clouds and Stennerskeugh Clouds, visited on walk 4. Look into Uldale once again and then enjoy the long view down the Rawthey valley to Sedbergh. To the west lie the rounded tops and steep-sided slopes of other fells.

Continue on, striding gently downhill, steadily descending right to rejoin the footpath that you walked just beyond Adamthwaite Sike. This grassy trod winds round the skirts of Wandale Hill and above the deserted Mountain View farmhouse. If you find the slope too steep, continue to a gate in the wall (but do not pass through) and then drop right to join the path, which continues through a lower gate in the wall.

Beyond, continue on a pleasing grassy track, with a wall to the right, to pass through another gate. This gives access to the grooved track taken above Narthwaite, almost at the outset of the walk. Descend to the farm. Go through the gate and turn right to pass through the next one. Bear right and descend the track to cross the ford again. Turn left and follow the track back to Cautley.

Cautley Crag

Walk 10: Kensgriff and Yarlside

Cross Keys Inn – Narthwaite – above Mountain View,
Westerdale – Spen Gill – Stockless Gill – Kensgriff –
Yarlside – Ben End – Cautley

Start/finish:	The wide verge beyond the Cross Keys Inn, Cautley on the A683, 4 miles north-east of Sedbergh (GR 698969).
Type of walk:	This 5-miler, short in distance but with considerable height gain, is one of the most enjoyable in the Howgills. It passes through the delightful Westerdale, in May full of the birdsong of migrants who have just arrived. It explores the delightful Spens Gill, in spring the banks of its beck lined with primroses. On the slopes above thrives the pretty mountain pansy. The climb up Kensgriff is generally easy but Yarlside presents a greater challenge, though it is less arduous than it looks, particularly if you bear steadily right as you climb. The view from both the cairns on both the summits is worth all the effort. The descent seems to go on and on but with no difficulties – there are fine views of Cautley Spout and the valley below to encourage you on your way.
Map:	OS Outdoor Leisure 19 Howgill Fells and Upper Eden Valley

The Walk

From the parking area, descend the steps to cross the footbridge over the River Rawthey. Pause as you go to look for dippers, sandpipers and goosanders. Beyond (as for walk 9) walk on to a T-junction of paths and turn right. Continue on the pleasing track, beside which fell ponies often graze.

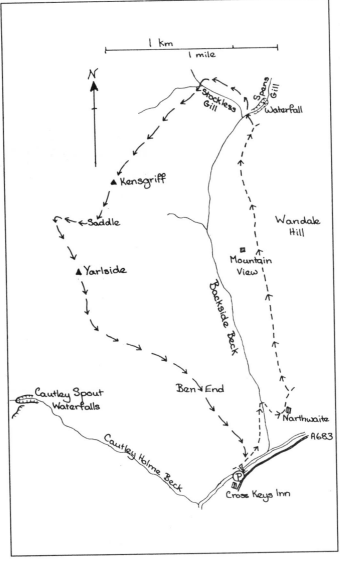

Follow the track as it swings left, with larches to the right. Cross the ford over Backside Beck on boulders (or wade) and climb the track beyond. Go through a gate and follow the track as it veers left. Beyond more gates, turn left to pass between two barns of Narthwaite Farm, just before the farmhouse on the right.

Ignore the good farm track on the left and continue ahead, climbing a rough track to two gates. Pass through the one on the left and continue on beside a wall to your left. Ahead is Kensgriff and to your left, over the tree-lined Backside Beck, stands Yarlside. This walk takes you across the saddle that links the two.

Go through the gate taken on your return from Wandale (walk 9). Follow the track as it passes above the deserted Mountain View farmhouse. In spring, look in the wet flushes as you go for golden saxifrage, milkmaids and penny cress.

Stride the clear track, and where it disappears under spongy sphagnum stroll on. As the track improves and swings right towards Adamthwaite, leave it by a narrow, grassy path on the left, which is easy to miss. Aim for the small, attractive waterfalls in Stockless Gill, one of the feeder streams of Backside Beck.

Pause in this quiet hollow and look right to see Spens Gill, which you might be tempted to

Spens Gill (Upper Fall)

explore. Its sides support several rowans which find a foothold in the cracks of the exposed rock.

Climb out of the gill and stay high on the slopes to the right of Stockless Gill. As you keep parallel with the stream, on your left, look for mountain pansies spangling the turf. Continue to the junction of the Stockless with another stream and descend the easy slope to step across both small becks.

Ascend the short, steepish slope ahead and then over some wettish mat grass and sphagnum, continuing always upwards. Join a narrow green path coming in on your right from the lower slopes of Randygill Top, which is the tall fell to your right. To the left you can see Wandale (walk 9) and your approach route, above Mountain View Farm. Ahead, and right, you can see Hazel Gill, descended on walk 31. Then you have your first glimpse of Bowderdale.

Mountain pansies

The clear path brings you unerringly to the small cairn on Kensgriff 1883ft (574m). Where did the stones come from? One has 'Ken' carved into it. Look for your first view of Ingleborough, often still snow-topped in late spring.

Continue on and descend to the saddle seen from across the valley on your outward walk. If by this time you need an escape route, you can turn left and follow a narrow path that takes you across the lower slopes of Yarlside to the side of the fell wall. Go on beside it and, where it turns left down the hillside, continue ahead, gently descending around Ben End to return to the footbridge over the Rawthey.

To continue on the planned walk to the summit of Yarlside, 2097ft (639m) you ascend its eastern face, which rears up before you. The easiest way is to bear steadily right as you climb. The turf is stepped because of landslip and these steps form natural narrow terraces that become easier as you climb.

Pause halfway up to look down the whole length of Bowderdale (walk 31). At your next pause you should be able to see Cross Fell. And then the large flattish top is reached. Turn left (south), and walk the narrow path to the summit cairn.

The view is extensive. Look right for the bridlepath from Bowderdale (walk 11) heading over the slopes on its way towards The Calf. To your left you can look down on Stennerskeugh and Fell End Clouds (walk 4), and above them Wild Boar Fell (walk 5). To its south is the long wedge of Swarth Fell. You can also see Ingleborough again and Pen-y-ghent.

From the cairn begin your descent, with Cautley Crag coming into view followed by the lovely falls of Cautley Spout. (This is the point at which to take your photographs.) At a second lower summit you are confronted by two paths. Take the left one to avoid the Screes. Continue on this half-left way to descend over Ben End. You can now see the wall that would have guided you if you needed the escape route. Descend over the springy turf, aiming for the footbridge over the Rawthey which has been in view for most of the way from the lower summit.

Walk 11: Cautley Spout – The Calf – Calders

Cross Keys – Cautley Spout – The Calf – Bram Rigg Top –
Calders – Settlebeck Gill – Underbank – Ellerthwaite –
Fawcett Bank – Rooker Gill – Cautley

Start/finish:	The wide verge beyond the Cross Keys Inn, Cautley on the A683, 4 miles north-east of Sedbergh (GR 698969).
Type of walk:	This is a strenuous, challenging high hill walk with a very steep climb to start. The return is mainly by low level paths, but they present a long, gradual uphill return to Cautley. It should not be attempted in doubtful weather and is dangerous in mist. Choose one of those long, sunny summer days. At 10 to 11 miles in length, and taking 6 to 7 hours to accomplish, this is the longest walk in the book.
Map:	OS Outdoor Leisure 19 Howgill Fells and Upper Eden Valley

The Walk

The Cross Keys Inn, Cautley has changed very little in its 400-year history. The National Trust acquired the former public house in 1949 under the will of Mrs E.A.Bunney, a staunch Methodist, who stipulated the property remain an unlicensed hotel. But alcohol is not completely banned; diners and guests are free to bring their own bottles of wine to have with their meals.

Before you start, look up the valley of Cautley Holme Beck to Cautley Spout, where the lively stream makes its descent of 800ft (244m) in sheer, foaming falls and cascades.

Leave the parking area by a signposted path, over shallow steps, leading sharply downwards under ash and sycamore to a footbridge

over the River Raw-
they. Beyond the
bridge, bear left along a
distinct path which
follows the route of the
river.

Continue along the
path as it swings right
away from the Raw-
they to continue up-
stream, and to the right
of Cautley Holme
Beck. Ahead lies Caut-
ley Crag, razor-edged
and impressive. To the
right lie the slopes of
Yarlside (walk 10). A
gently climbing stroll
along a good path
brings you to the foot
of the falls.

Cautley Spout

Prepare for a scram-
ble up the very steep slope, or if this is too daunting use the winding
path, through bracken, up on your right and then contour back again
above the falls.

From the rough, narrow path, with extreme care, look down on
the lovely beck, racing below rowan, holly, birch and ash. Rock
gardens suppport mosses and ferns, and ivy, with bright, shiny
leaves, trails down the limestone rock face. In summer, angelica,
hardheads and lady's mantle thrive. Take regular pauses to look
back down to the green fields, bordered with dark green hedges, on
the other side of the River Rawthey. Beyond, moorland stretches
away to the foot of Baugh Fell.

From above the falls do not cross the stream but go on ascending
to join the grooved path coming out of Bowderdale (seen on Walk
10). Follow this (west) across the plateau, coming close to a small

tarn. Then make a short detour, left (south), to the trig point on The Calf 2,218ft (676m), the highest point in the Howgills. Stand on the summit for superb all-round views to the Lakeland hills, to Morecambe Bay, to the Pennines, and to Yorkshire and the familiar shapes of the Three Peaks.

From the The Calf, walk (south) on a wide track over the flat summit of Bram Rigg Top and, still heading south, on to Calders on

a wide, stony track, an airy highway with breathtaking views on both sides. Use your map regularly here.

Continue along the path as it comes close to a wire boundary fence. Turn right, walking with the fence to your left, to go over the cairned summit of Calders. The track then turns sharp left for a steep descent, with grand views into Hobdale Gill

Head on along the good path, with Arant Haw to the right, and then, at the first cairn, turn left onto a narrower path. Go on down the grassy path, which descends rapidly for nearly a mile, keeping parallel to the beck on your left as it hurries down Settlebeck Gill. Pass through the kissing gate in the fell wall.

Continue downhill, with the delightful tree-lined gill to your left. Do not climb the next stile but cross the beck, with a little boulder hopping, and continue on down the lovely path to the three-armed signpost at Castlehaw Farm.

Hardheads and Ladies' Mantle

If the beck is in spate then go through the stile, ignored above, and walk on to a gated gap stile. Beyond, stroll on a good track to pass two pleasing barns. Where the track swings right, turn left to

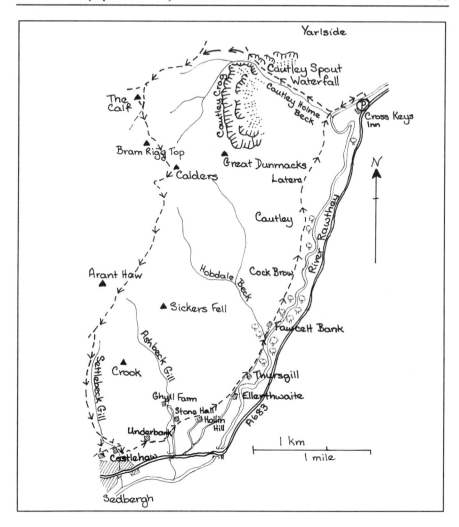

pass between more barns and a dwelling. Climb some steps to a gated gap stile in the wall.

Beyond, walk ahead following a green track across a meadow to Castlehaw Farm. Go through the buildings, following the arrow, and turn right over a small bridge to a three-armed signpost. Go on ahead in the direction of Ghyll Farm, and after 45 metres look for the gap stile in the wall on the right, opposite a farm building. Beyond, cross a small meadow and a stile into a larch wood. Step over a small stream to another stile and walk on along a path which leads to a gate and a signposted reinforced track. Turn left and dawdle along the tree-lined way to Underbank.

Follow the track through dwellings at Underbank and pass through a gate on the right. Walk down the lane for 18 metres to a signposted stile on the left. Walk straight ahead to a stile and footbridge in the far left corner. Walk on, keeping a wall to the right, to a gate, and a stone stile beside it. These lead you onto a farm road.

Turn left and walk in front of the gracious Stone Hall. Pass through the farm gate on the right and walk eastwards, keeping close to the stone wall on the left. Cross the footbridge, climb the ladder-stile at the end of it and walk on to a gate to Hollin Hill Farm. Beyond a lovely old barn, pass through a gate. This is the main highway for the cows so pick your way carefully.

Carry on across the pasture to a ladder stile in the far right corner. Cross the meadow ahead to a stile. Then keep to the left side of a wall that ends in the middle of the field and walk to a stile on the right. Press on in front of Ellerthwaite to a rickety stile to Buckbank Lane. Turn left.

Proceed up the lane to Thursgill. Notice the quaint porch with T.H 1855 written above it and notice, also, the excellent cobbled farmyard. Pass through the gate at the end of the yard and continue along the track. Amble through the lovely wooded gorge of Iseman's Dub, with the Rawthey flowing through it far below. Cross the signposted small, stone bridge over Hobdale Beck and climb the steep, reinforced track past the neat dwelling at Fawcett Bank.

Follow the yellow waymarks along the fellside, with the Rawthey flowing along the valley bottom. Keep to the same contour along well-trodden paths, and above the wire fence that stretches for nearly a mile. Above the path, bracken sweeps up Cock Brow, Cautley and Latera.

Then the path drops downhill, beneath trees, to lower pastures. Cross the footbridge over Cautley Holme Beck and follow the path, taken earlier, to the footbridge over the Rawthey and up to the Cross Keys Inn.

Walk 12: Knott and Sickers Fell

Sedbergh – Castlehaw Farm – Ashbeck Gill – Little Ashbeck
Gill – Knott – Sickers Fell – Ashbeck Gill – side of Crook –
Settlebeck Gill – Sedbergh

Start/finish: Loftus Hill free car park, Sedbergh (GR 656920)

Type of walk: A pleasing 5-miler over pastures and then onto fell
slopes. All the climbs are gently graded and the
views from the cairns of the two tops are expan-
sive and dramatic. Choose a good day. It is not a
walk for rainy or misty weather. Go in late spring
when the fells resound to the calls of curlews and
the songs of skylarks and meadow pipits.

Map: OS Outdoor Leisure 19 Howgill Fells and Upper
Eden Valley

The Walk

Turn right out of the car park and then right again into Back Lane
(labelled at its far end!) in the direction of Brough. Once beyond the
junction with Main Street, which comes in on your left, and just into
Long Lane, cross the road and take the steps to the gated stile, which
gives access to a meadow.

Stride the metalled path, with Castlehaw and the motte and bailey
to your left. Cross the footbridge over Settlebeck Gill and turn left
to pass the intriguing crenellated Thorns, once a lodge to Thorns
Hall. It was built in the 16th century and has been added to.

Continue on for a dozen or more paces to pass through a gate to
a track, on your left, signposted 'to the fell'. Continue beside trees,
with the pretty beck also to your left. Take the narrow, signposted
path leading off the track to a stile into a shady copse. Cross the beck
and climb the steps to emerge from the trees by another stile.

Walk towards the stile ahead but do not take it. Instead veer right

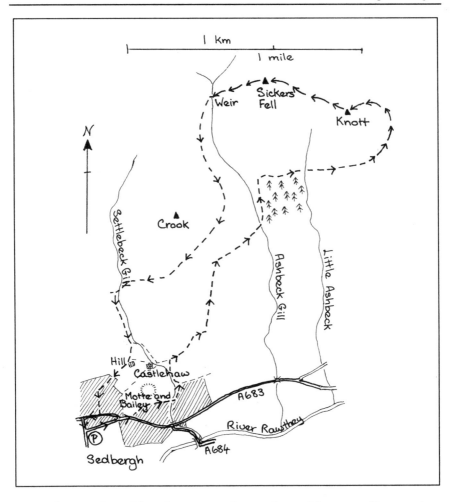

towards a track and head on towards a pylon with power lines going from it in several directions. Once beyond the pylon, keep parallel with the fence and hawthorns on your right to come to a stile in the far right corner, where several fences come together.

Go over the stile and continue to a sturdy gate beside a barn. Beyond, turn left to stride a gently rising pasture to climb another stile. Bear right to pass between straggly hawthorns and then climb the steeply rising pasture to a stile in the top right corner taking you through the fell wall.

Turn right, and after a short muddy patch the high, airy path becomes a grassy delight. Pause to enjoy glimpses into Garsdale, the Rawthey valley and shadowy Dentdale. Stride on the clear path, keeping parallel with the wall, in the direction of a walled conifer plantation. Follow the steepish grassy trod as it curves down the slope to the side of Ashgill Beck. Cross on convenient boulders and climb the opposite bank. Turn left and begin a steady, but unrelenting ascent, with the wall and the dense conifers to your right.

At the corner of the wall, go with it as it turns right and continue

on to pass another plantation. Just beyond the last of the trees, look down right to see a delightful corner where a stone sheepfold stands, close to the beck, surrounded by heavily blossoming gorse. Sometimes it is possible, here, to see a merlin flying fast and low between the bushes.

Merlin

Step across Little Ashbeck Gill and stride on a wide, rising grassy way over the skirts of Knott. Follow it as it spirals left, and upwards, and brings you to the cairn standing at 1407 ft (429m). Here you will want to pause to enjoy the view. In spring listen for the calls of pipits and curlews.

From the cairn, bear west to a flattish area where Little Ashbeck Gill makes an uncertain start on its journey down the valley. To your right (north), at the foot of Middle Tongue, you can sometimes see long-tailed, black fell ponies grazing. Occasionally they frolic and gambol across the pasture. West of Middle Tongue lies the austere Hobdale Gill, and to the east of the Tongue you can see the awesome Grimes Head Gill.

Join the grassy way that climbs right for a hundred metres or so and then leave it to climb, left, up the rough pasture to come to the cairn on the flat summit of Sickers Fell, 1634 ft (498m). Look north-east to see Fell End Clouds on Wild Boar Fell, east towards Ingleborough and west towards Arnside Knott and Morecambe Bay.

Leave the cairn, walking west over the flat top, to look down on Ashbeck Gill. Descend the grassy slopes, aiming for a grassy, table-like overhang just above the beck. A narrow path to the left of this 'table' leads down to a small weir. Step across the beck and join the narrow path leading left, downstream. In places you can see the pipeline heading down the valley, carrying water for Sedbergh.

Continue along the path, which soon becomes a wide, grassy way. As the path climbs steadily, look left to see a sheepfold and sheep-wash below. Stroll on the now narrowing path as it continues, winding right along the skirts of Crook. (This path was walked in the opposite direction on walk 13.) From here you can see much of Sedbergh stretched out along the river.

On approaching Settlebeck Gill the path peters out. Walk on with the wall now close on your left. Follow the wall on an intermittent path as it turns left. Several rocky paths lead to the water's edge. Look for the continuing path opposite and cross the stream at the most convenient place.

Climb up left to a fine iron kissing gate in the fell wall. Here you might be tempted to have a pause on the seat, just before the gate, strategically placed for enjoying the Rawthey Valley and the town.

Pass through the gate and continue downhill beside the beck on your left. Climb a stile, which has a splendid dog gate. Stride the short, hedged track beyond, to pass through a gated stile. Continue down the track, passing two barns on your left. Then follow the track as it swings right. Beyond the gate, walk the paved road and continue with it as it swings left and descends to Main Street.

Turn right and continue past the pleasing shops to the corner of Finkle Street, where you turn left to walk on to the car park.

Walk 13: Crook and Arant Haw

Sedbergh – Settlebeck Gill – Crook – Arant Haw – Nab –
Crosdale Beck – Lockbank Farm – Sedbergh

Start/finish:	Loftus Hill free car park, Sedbergh (GR 656920)
Type of walk:	An exhilarating 5½ mile walk to two delightful fells. The walk to the waterfall in Settlebeck Gill, taking you through pastures and along a pleasing hedged path, contrasts sharply with the continuing route over the rolling fells. Once you are across the beck and up a steep slope, a gently graded grassy path leads you towards Ashbeck Gill. There follows a short climb to the top of Crook, 1509ft (460m), with its pleasing views of the town. Then comes a pathless trek over rough pasture and a short, steepish climb to the top of Arant Haw 1985ft (605m), from where there are wonderful views of the Lune Valley and Morecambe Bay. The descent over the Nab is one of the Howgills best strolls, with even more delightful views. The return is along the fell wall.
Map:	OS Outdoor Leisure 19 Howgill Fells and Upper Eden Valley

The Walk

Turn right out of the car park, and walk on to the main street, with its interesting and varied shops. Turn right and then left into Joss Lane, with its car park to your right. Continue upwards and follow the road where it bears right, to pass through a gate at its end. Walk on along a track, taking the higher way where it branches, leaving Hill farm and its barns to your right. Stride on upwards, with the wall to your right, to pass through stiles, continuing with Settlebeck

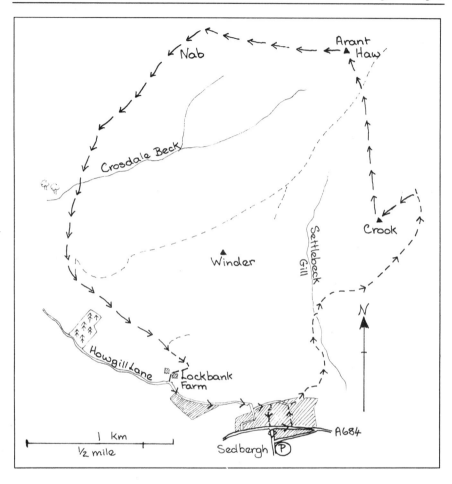

Gill now to your right. A splendid kissing gate gives access to the
fell – and a seat on which to sit to get your breath back.

Then take the path that descends delightfully to the waterfall on
the beck. Cross just above it on convenient stones and then climb
up on a grassy trod, through bracken, to come close to the fell wall.

Ignore the continuing way by the wall and take a narrow, rising
path going on along the lower slopes of Crook. The very straight way
crosses the breast of the fell, sometimes over scree and sometimes
with a steep slope downwards as it continues to rise. Gradually it
swings round north, with wild and steep Ashbeck Gill to your right.

Go on until you reach a clear division of paths. Here take the left branch, a grooved way that climbs steadily to the ridge. To attain Crook's summit cairn, bear left, steadily climbing. After enjoying the view of the town (south), look north and slightly west to see Arant Haw (often known as Higher Winder). Between you and Arant Haw lies pathless fell, beyond which a grassy track can be seen ascending straight to its summit. Head across the wide, flat ridge, keeping to the higher ground, to the well walked track that links Sedbergh with The Calf (see walk 11). Cross this and begin your fairly easy ascent of Arant Haw.

Sheepfold by Crosdale Back, below Nab

From the summit, northwards, you can see Calders, Bram Rigg Top and The Calf. Crook seems a small protuberance. Turn left (west) from the top and begin the glorious descent of the wide ridge, walking a wide grassy trod. Continue over two small rises and then, where the way divides, bear left (southwest) to continue your descent of Nab.

Aim left for a corner in the fell wall. Below, to the left of the wall, is Crosdale Beck, which you ford or step over just above a small waterfall. Stroll on for nearly a mile along a grassy trod, with the fell wall to your right and the slopes of Winder to your left. You step across several tiny streams along the pleasing way.

At Lockbank Farm turn right through a gate in the wall. Continue ahead through the yard and on to a narrow access lane. At Howgill Lane, turn left. Stride on and take the first left turn, at the area named Havera. Walk the quiet road and take the signposted ginnel on the right. Cross another road and continue on through a second ginnel to reach Sedbergh's main street. Walk ahead to regain the car park.

Walk 14: Winder from Sedbergh

Sedbergh – Lockbank Farm -Winder – Lockbank Farm –
Settlebeck Gill – Castlehaw Farm – Sedbergh

Start/finish: Loftus Hill free car park, Sedbergh (GR 656920)

Type of walk: All the family will enjoy this delightful 3 to 4 mile
walk to Winder 1552 ft (473m), which stands
proudly above Sedbergh. Wonderful grassy paths
lead unerringly to the small summit, with its white-
painted trig point. The return is across Winder's
breast, on an even more delectable track. An ex-
tension added to this walk takes you along the fell
wall and then descends through pastures and
hedged ways to view, over a pasture, Sedbergh's
motte and bailey.

Map: OS Outdoor Leisure 19 Howgill Fells and Upper
Eden Valley

The Walk

Talk to Sedbergh folk and they speak about Winder as if it were in
their own backyard – though of course it does overlook most of their
backyards. They delight in telling you the best route and how it is
impossible to get lost. There are several signposts on the way
through the roads and lanes which direct you to The Fell, which
means Winder, their fell.

Turn right out of the car park, and walk ahead to the main street,
which you cross. Turn left and almost immediately take a signposted
ginnel between houses. Cross a quiet road and continue on along
another ginnel, signposted 'Public footpath via fell'. At its end turn
left and walk on to Howgill Lane. Turn right to pass another signpost
directing you to 'The fell'.

Stroll on to the derestriction sign to take the next right turn,

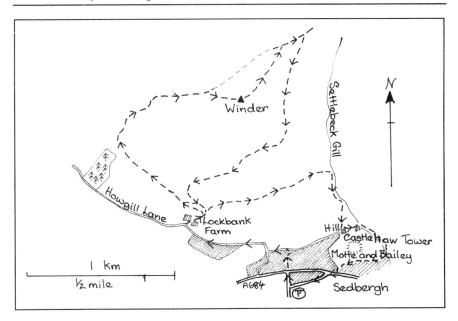

signposted 'Permissive road to the fell'. The delightful walled lane leads to Lockbank Farm. Follow the blue arrow in the farmyard that directs you right. Walk the short walled track to the fell gate.

Beyond, walk left beside the fell wall. Continue ahead, ignoring a steeply climbing path going off right (this is your return route). Go on parallel to, but at a distance from, the wall, choosing the main grassy track and aiming towards the tops of the trees in Nursery Wood.

Step across a small beck, then another, and then a narrow ditch. Bear right to wind round a small knoll to take a path on the right, heading straight up the fell slope, a grassy trod through bracken.

There are many grassy trods and tracks, but keep your eye on the highest point on Winder and head along the widest, which leads you to the trig point with a small cairn beyond. Pause here and enjoy the great panorama of the Lune valley, the Lakeland hills and glistening Morecambe Bay.

Stroll on along the pleasing track and at the first small cairn turn right to walk a delightful terrace-like path. Soon Sedbergh comes into view, with Garsdale to its left and Dentdale beyond. Follow the track as it winds round right (west), descending all the time on a gentle gradient. Finally, it swings left and descends sharply to the gate in the fell wall. There is a seat here where you might wish to pause to make a choice, either to retrace your steps through the farmyard and on into the town, or to return by a more rambling route. To do this turn left and walk along beside the fell wall.

The grassy track is a pleasure to walk and eventually brings you to the edge of Settlebeck Gill and its pleasing waterfall. There are two more seats here. Go through the kissing gate on your right and walk on beside the lovely tree-lined beck. Climb the next stile, which is at the right end of a short wall – notice its intricately designed dog gate. Go on to a gated gap stile and then continue, with a wall to your left, along a track. Stride on to pass a pleasing barn. Here the track bears right. The walk continues left (very easy to miss this left turn), passing between a barn on the left and a dwelling on the right. Climb some steps and go through a gated gap stile. Stride ahead across the pasture, towards Castlehead Farm.

To your right, looming upwards through the trees, is a flat-topped hill, with a conical mound on it. The flat-topped hill may have given its name to Sedbergh. In Old Norse 'Setberg' means flat-topped hill.

Winder from Sedburgh

On the OS map it is named Castlehaw Tower. The Normans built their motte and bailey castle on the flat top.

At the farm, follow the arrow directing you left. Cross the stone bridge over the beck to a three-armed signpost. Go on in the direction of Ghyll Farm and, in a few paces and opposite the next barn, take the stile in the wall on your right. Cross a pasture to a stile into a copse of larch. Follow the steps down to step across the beck and climb the next stile. Walk downhill on the good path to a gate to a track. Turn right to walk below Castlehaw Tower, with just a glimpse of the motte and bailey.

Look for the signposted footpath on the right that directs you behind houses and continues over a small green to the road, which you cross. Walk on, right, with playing fields to your left. At the road end, turn left to rejoin your car.

Walk 15: Sedbergh – Brigflatts

Sedbergh – Underbank – Stone Hall – Straight Bridge –
River Rawthey – New Bridge – Millthrop – Archers Hall –
Birks Mill – A683 – Brigflatts – Birks – Sedbergh

Start/finish:	Loftus Hill free car park, Sedbergh (GR 656920)
Type of Walk:	A generally level 7-miler through the pleasing countryside around Sedbergh. For much of the time you keep company with the River Rawthey, a particularly glorious stretch on this walk. There are many stiles to climb and squeeze through, which seem to have been constructed by someone very tall and thin; if you take a rucksack, heave it over before attempting to pass through. For those stiles with a high first step (on both sides) a walking pole is of great help.
Map:	OS Outdoor Leisure 19 Howgill Fells and Upper Eden Valley

The Walk

Turn right out of the car park and right again to pass Sedbergh School's library. It was originally the school house, built in 1716. Continue along the Brough road. Just beyond where the main street comes in on the left, cross the road, with care, to take the signposted, stiled footpath through the wall.

Beyond, walk the reinforced path, with houses to your right and the wooded Castlehaw Tower with its motte and bailey to your left. Cross the footbridge and turn left. Notice the house named Thorns to your right, with its turreted round tower.

Ignore the left turn and go on the wide reinforced track, signposted Underbank. Follow the way as it passes between houses and through a waymarked gate. Beyond look for the signpost, directing you left through a stile beside a gate. Head straight across the pasture to take a hidden, stiled footbridge over Ash Beck. Stroll on with the wall to your right to take a narrow stepped stile to the right of a gate.

Once through, turn left to walk the metalled track to pass in front of Stone Hall, which lies on your left. This lovely house has many small, stone mullioned windows, and its chimneys are square with round pots. Turn right through a waymarked gate and walk ahead, with the wall to your right.

Stride on with a hawthorn hedge now to your right and keep on the way, curving left, with the line of hawthorns guiding you, to a small stile on your right beside Little Ashbeck. Walk downstream and after 15 or so paces, cross the beck to take a stile into a pasture.

Go on downstream, with the beck to your right, to a sturdy but high-stepped, stone stile to a narrow road. Cross and take the stile opposite. Stride ahead to another high- stepped stile onto the A683.

Turn left and walk the verge for 275 metres. Cross the A-road and, just before Straight Bridge, take the stiled steps. Join the path, with the River Rawthey to your left. Watch out for mallards and mergansers as you stroll the delightful way. A notice asks you to remain on the narrow path beside the river bank.

As you climb a ladder of steps to continue, look left to see the River Clough descending in pleasing cascades before it unites with the Rawthey. Go on the stiled way beside the tree-lined river, which leads to a path close to the hurrying water, with a wall to the right. Here the sheep cannot get at the vegetation and the footpath, in spring, is lined with a plethora of wild flowers.

Stride a footbridge to join the A684. Turn left and cross Settlebeck Bridge, with its huge cutwater. Take the continuing signposted footpath to walk beside the Rawthey, flowing sweetly to your right. Enjoy this pleasing reach of the river and stroll on to join the road to Dent.

Cross the road with care and look down on the river. Here, at the right time of the year, you should see a pair of dippers which regularly nest in a hole high up in the stonework of the fine bridge.

Do not cross the bridge, but take the short, narrow left turn to

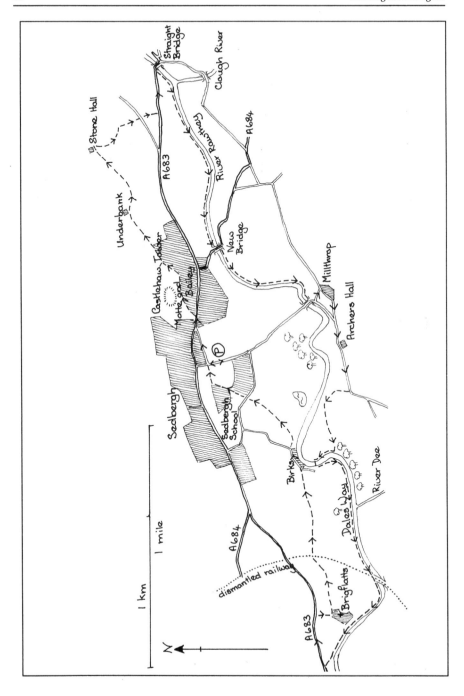

Millthrop. At the T-junction, turn right to pass through the attractive hamlet and go on to join the road to Dent, which can be busy. Pass Archers Hall on the left (1681). It has mullioned windows and a studded oak door.

Continue with great care on the narrow road, which has no convenient verge, to take a signposted path on the right, just where the road swings left. Climb the ladderstile ahead and stride a wide, walled track. Follow the wall on the left as it swings left and continue to pass through a gate. Go on the well waymarked way until you reach the bank of the Rawthey once more.

Turn right. After 135 metres, look for the narrow path dropping down towards the river and the start of the fine wooden footbridge across this dramatic reach. On the far side of the bridge is Birks Mill, once a cotton mill, where you can still see some of the old buildings.

Turn left and take the signposted footpath, Rawthey Way, which runs close to the chuckling river. In spring this path is lined with violets, primroses and wood rush. Stroll on the delightful path. Climb a stile into an oak and beech woodland, from where you can see the River Dee join the Rawthey in a flurry of foam as both rivers rage over huge ribs of rock.

Saunter on the high, level way, now

Primroses and violets

Iron Bridge over Rawthey

with the river well below, to a flight of steps which gives access to a disused railway track. Cross and descend to a pasture to continue beside the Rawthey. After about 90 metres, look back to see the magnificent iron bridge that once carried the old Ingleton-Tebay railway line of the London North Western Railway over the river. It was closed to passengers in 1953.

Go on along the riverside, following the signed way. The path then climbs gently to pass a farm and then higher still above a dramatic stretch of the Rawthey, where wild flowers proliferate. The pleasing way brings you to a stile to the A683.

Turn right and walk with care along the hedged road for 320 metres towards Brigflatts and the Quaker Meeting House. As you go, look left to see restored Ingmire Hall. In the 1680s it was the home of the Catholic Otway family. When the Quakers were being persecuted, Sir John Otway, who had great sympathy for them, would use his influence to have local Friends released from various prisons to return home to help with the harvest.

Turn right into the signposted narrow lane, which leads to Brigflatts and Birks. As you approach the houses, a former flax-weavers' settlement, look over the wall on the right to see the Quaker burial ground, with its rows of identical simple headstones about which in spring, daffodils flower in great abundance.

Continue on to visit the meeting house which was constructed in 1675. It is set in a picturesque garden full of flowers and birdsong. Pass through the oak, studded door. Wooden stairs lead to a gallery where the womenfolk sat, safe from any trouble that might have arisen from persecutors. Look for the dog pen where Friends could leave their dogs. Pause awhile to enjoy the peace to be found in the house and in the garden.

Return along the lane to take the signposted gate for Birks, opposite the burial ground. Walk ahead to take two stiles and then bear slightly left towards the disused railway track, passing under a well waymarked bridge. Stride on, with the wall to your left. When it turns away left, head on for a gate and take the gap stile to the right of it.

Cross an access track to climb another stile. Stroll on to the step stile in the far right corner. Go on to the next stile. Beyond, keep beside the hedge on the right and then over a short stretch of pasture to a signposted gate on the right, which gives on to a narrow lane at Birks.

Turn left and walk through the hamlet to take a kissing gate on the right, signposted Rawthey Way. Stay on the continuing track as it winds round left, keeping close to the wall of Birks House. Beyond a kissing gate (in pieces on the ground), strike across a field to go through a kissing gate in the far right corner onto a narrow lane.

Turn left and walk to the road. Cross and pass through the kissing gate opposite. Climb the slope to go through the next kissing gate. Beyond follow the track as it swings right and returns you to the car park.

Walk 16: Castley – The Calf

Parking area – Four Lane Ends – Castley – White Fell –
The Calf – Bram Rigg Top – Seat Knott – Birkhaw –
Howgill – Parking area

Start/finish: Finding a parking space for this walk is very difficult. The lane heading west from Four Lane Ends
towards Lowgill has several passing places which
must, of course, be avoided, but there are two
slightly smaller areas that could be used. Or you
could start as for walk 17 and stride for just over
a mile, each way, to and from Four Lane Ends (GR
631958 or GR 615966). Another choice might be
Fairmile Gate, as for walk 18 (GR 628982). Four
Lane Ends lies 1½ miles south along Howgill Lane.

Type of walk: This route provides 6¼ miles of glorious walking.
There are good grassy paths and tracks all the way
through this quiet, remote part of the Howgills.
The way goes unrelentingly up, but the ground
underfoot is a joy to tread, and the views are good
too. The summit of the Calf is reached by a gently
rising path. The return is made by the pleasing
grassy way down the slopes of Bram Rigg, with fine
views ahead over the Lune Gorge, into Lakeland
and to the coast. The final stretch takes you
through pastures and beside Smithy Beck, and
then skirts the hamlet of Howgill.

Map: OS Outdoor Leisure 19 Howgill Fells and Upper
Eden Valley

The Walk

At Four Lane Ends take the concrete track, rising towards the fells, signposted 'Bridleway to Bowderdale, 8 miles'. Walk the hedged way to Top Withens, named as Cookson's Tenement on the OS map.

Continue on to the three-armed signpost at Castley Farm. Here take the bridleway for 'The Calf, 2½ miles', the concrete track now replaced by a reinforced, walled way. Below to the right Chapel Beck hurries between its tree-lined banks.

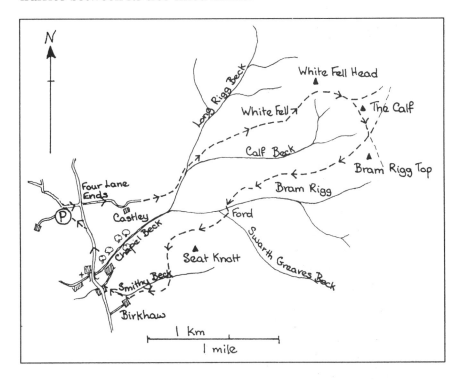

Pass through the gate and continue on a descending track that curves round Castley Knotts. As you go look down to see the confluence of Long Rigg Beck with Calf Beck; the resultant stream continues as Chapel Beck. Ford Long Rigg Beck at a convenient point, just above the confluence and where the reinforced track ends. Continue uphill on a wide grassy way to begin your ascent of White Fell. As you go, look across the ever deepening gill of Calf Beck to Bram Rigg to see the grassy track you will take on your return.

Soon the way continues as a grooved trod. Pause often on this

Lowgill Viaduct

lengthy climb to enjoy the views of other fells and to look back over
the path you have just trodden and westwards towards Lakeland
and the coast.

At the next brow, the upward climb continues. Just where the
main track levels off and begins to swing right (east), a narrow trod
leads off left (north) for White Fell Head 2087ft (636m), a flattish
grassy area from where you can see Yarlside and Hazelgill Knott
(walks 10 and 31).

The way to The Calf goes on as a path and then swings gently right
along the wide ridge. To your right is the great hollow on the sheer
sides of which rises Calf Beck. And then the trig point, 2218ft (676m)
lies ahead, white and welcoming.

Continue on a wide way for 275 metres, and at the first depression
take the narrow path, leading off right, along the rim of the great
hollow and on the side of Bram Rigg. Or you may prefer to ascend
to the broad top of Bram Rigg, 2205ft (672m), and then begin your
descent on a grassy way. The two paths meet to continue down the
delightful ridge. The views ahead are magnificent, and on either side
you look down on Calf Beck and Bram Rigg Beck, snaking through
their steep-sided gills.

Watch out for the track branching left just after a sheepfold. Go
on down and down to join a reinforced track which swings left and
then right to the side of Bram Rigg Beck, which you ford. Bear right
along the wide cart track to pass a well-built sheepfold. Cross Swarth
Greaves Beck and begin your climb up the slope on the continuing
track to skirt Seat Knott.

Stride on as the way swings left, with a wall to your right. Ford two narrow becks and then pass through two gates close to each other. Go on beside the wall and then take the next gate on the right. A good track continues on, with a wall to the right and a view of Lowgill viaduct. Pass through a gate to continue on with Smithy Beck to your right, hurrying through its gill.

Follow the track, which is shadowed by larch, to Birkhaw Farm. Here take a gate on the right immediately before the farmhouse (up against the side wall of the dwelling). Go on down the pasture, with trees to the right, to a stile. Press on to the next stile and continue to Smithy Cottage, once a forge, where you turn right to walk Howgill Lane.

As you approach Chapel Beck Bridge, you might wish to visit the church (see walk 17) in the small hamlet and look for salmon leaping the rocks under the bridge on their way to spawn higher up the beck.

Salmon leaping

To continue, go on up the lane to pass the old school and on to Gate Side Farm. Pass through the gate on the left, beyond the last building. Bear right across the pasture to take the first of five stiles that take you back to the lane where you have hopefully found a place to park.

To reach the parking area beyond the viaduct, turn left. If you have parked at Fairmile Gate remain on the lane from the hamlet of Howgill.

Walk 17: Lowgill – Fox's Pulpit – Howgill

Lowgill – High House -Fox's Pulpit – River Lune – Howgill – Crook of Lune Bridge – Lowgill

Start/finish: A grassy verge opposite the telephone box at Beckfoot, on the B6257, west of the defunct Lowgill viaduct (GR 615966). The tiny hamlet, also known as Lowgill, lies south of the junction of the B-road with the A685.

Type of walk: This pleasing 6-mile walk starts from the tiny hamlet, where time seems to have stood still. In sharp contrast, close by, the most modern of vehicles hurtle along the M6 through the Lune Gorge, almost cheek by jowl with trains on the railway. Soon their disconcerting noise is left behind as the way continues into the quiet pastures of Firbank Fell. After leaving the lonely preaching stone known as Fox's Pulpit, the way descends steadily to the lovely Lune and on to the great delight of the walk, the settlement of Howgill – a pilgrimage for all those who wish to know the hub of this book of walks about the hills named after it.

Map: OS Outdoor Leisure 19 Howgill Fells and Upper Eden Valley

The Walk

Leave the parking area and walk the narrow lane, part of the Dales Way, with the telephone box and the viaduct to your left. Take the well signposted left turn in the centre of the hamlet. Cross the beck and go by Half-Island House to climb a hedged and grassy track. Continue on the sunken way.

At the end of the track, leave the Dales Way and turn left to stroll beside a hedge. Pause by the gate to enjoy a grand view of the western

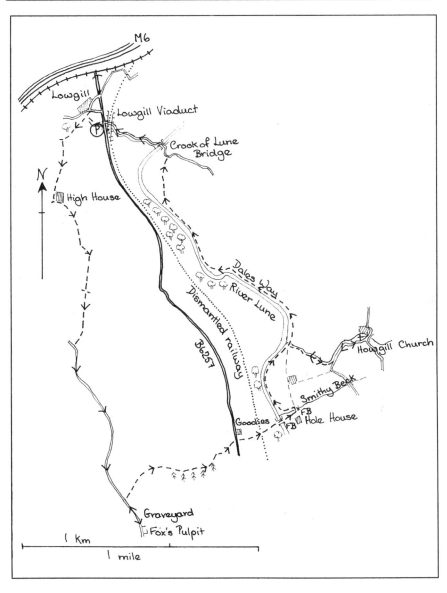

Howgills and of Lowgill viaduct – in winter a glorious rose-red sandstone against a backdrop of snow-covered mountains.

Go on by the hedge to pass through the next pasture and then to a gate that leads into another hedged track. At its end pass through the gate to High House Farm. Bear left to walk in front of the farmhouse and go through a blue gate to a walled track, with a barn to the right and a fine cottage to the left. Look for the datestones on both buildings.

Follow the curving track and, beyond the gate, continue beside the wall on the left to climb the stile in the far corner. Stride ahead to the next stile and go on descending gently. Cross duckboarding over a stream and take the stile in the wall on the left. Continue on the sunken track, now with the wall to your right, to Firbank Fell Lane. Turn left.

The quiet lane climbs, and then descends, with glorious views of the Howgills to lighten your step. Notice the signposted footpath on the left just before the cattle grid. This is the way the walk continues after visiting the preaching stone. To do this go on uphill to visit, first, the lonely walled churchyard where a solitary stone bears the carved names of William and Elizabeth Bentham, who died early in the nineteenth century. Four large larch, with limbs outstretched, huddle against the east wall. Railings protect a cuppressus from wandering sheep. Here stood the old Firbeck Chapel.

Beyond, take a ladder stile on the left that gives access to the foot of Fox's Pulpit, a huge, fissured, lichen-clad outcrop of natural rock. This is where the Quaker preached, in June 1652, to more than a thousand Seekers. Many had attended the Whitsun Fair at Sedbegh, and others the service in the old chapel.

Return over the cattle grid and take the stile, now on your right. Continue downhill – not too close to the fence and then the wall on your right, because of the bogginess of the ground. Climb the next stile and, walking beside a deep gill on the right, its slopes lined with larch, carry on to the next. A sunken track goes on down the slope. When it temporarily disappears, stride over a small pasture to pick it up again. It can be very wet here so remain on the right of the hedged way but move into it well before it joins the B6257.

Cross the B-road, take a gate on your right and walk ahead to the next gate (neither signposted). Beyond, descend the steep slope, where you might see roe deer grazing. Cross the dismantled railway and continue downhill to the fishermen's bridge over the River Lune.

Follow the path left to walk beside the gracious river. Then at the side of Smithy Beck, a small tributary, follow the path inland to the side of Hole House Farm. It is believed that Roger Lupton, the founder of Sedbergh School, was born here. Another family that lived here, at a later date, is said to have engaged in the slave trade and kept its 'wares' in chains in the cellar.

Take the footbridge across the beck and then pass through the gate. Turn left to follow the waymarks to return to the side of the River Lune. Stroll upstream to a three-armed signpost. Leave the Lune and head inland beside Chapel Beck in the direction of Howgill Lane and the settlement of Howgill.

The clear grassy way leads to a narrow, metalled lane where you bear right to walk into the hamlet. Here, until 1870, there was a woollen mill that employed many workers. Walk on through the green to Holy Trinity Church, built in 1836. Go inside and enjoy its simple charm. Look in the churchyard for the gravestones of the Herd family. Richard Herd wrote *Scraps of Poetry*, which includes a moving poem on a sheepdog helping a shepherd to rescue sheep trapped in snow. Then sit on the seat by the church door and enjoy the delightful scene.

Great Tit, in oak tree

The hamlet has given its name to the range of fells known as the Howgills. This came about when the cartographers of the Ordnance Survey found that though each of the fells had a name, the range did not. Beyond the church a gate gives access to Howgill Lane, and further north the continuing Fairmile Road. These form part of an old Roman road which continued to Tebay, past the site of a Roman camp.

Return through the hamlet to the three-armed signpost passed earlier. Cross the footbridge over Chapel Beck, and continue beside the Lune, on your left, in the direction of Crook of Lune Bridge.

Walk the path through oak woodland, sometimes close to the hurrying river and sometimes high above. Go on where the path becomes a grassy track. Look for your first sighting of the elegant viaduct, where you have parked.

A footpath sign directs you to the road. Turn left and cross the fine, five-hundred-year- old Crook of Lune Bridge, with its huge cutwaters. Carry on through the buildings known as Pool House, with pleasing cascades above. Pass under the eleven-arched viaduct to rejoin your car.

Crook of Lune Bridge

Walk 18: Fairmile Gate, Bram Rigg Top, The Calf and Fell Head

Fairmile Gate – Beck House – Castley Knotts – Sevy Rigg – Bram Rigg Top – The Calf – Height of Bush Howe – Breaks Head – Fell Head – Whin's End – Fairmile Gate

Start/finish: Fairmile Road (GR 628982). Fairmile Road, just over a mile long, is built on the site of a Roman road (see walk 17). The approach road from Tebay, at first narrow, has few passing places. It continues over narrow Carlingill Bridge and then through unenclosed fell. Park on the right, immediately before the first wall. A larger parking area lies 45 metres along on the opposite side. If you are approaching from Sedbergh, along narrow Howgill Lane, the parking areas lie just beyond Fairmile Bridge.

Type of walk: A glorious, 7½-mile challenging walk into the heart of the fells. You stroll tracks and paths and cross some pathless fell. On the steady climb of Bram Rigg to The Calf, give yourself time to pause and enjoy the immense quiet. The delightful ridge walk is interrupted by the need to descend a steepish gill before the steeper ascent to Breaks Head. Then follows another grand ridge path to Fell Head, from where you can peep into the gills and to the tops walked elsewhere in this book. The descent to Whin's End involves a steep downhill trek on a narrow grassy path. From the crest of the spur, a pathless beeline brings you back to your car.

Map: OS Outdoor Leisure 19 Howgills and Upper Eden Valley

The Walk

From the parking area walk south to cross Fairmile Beck Bridge and cattle grid (there is no longer a gate). Stroll the lovely lane for just over a mile. In summer it is lined with a colourful array of wild

flowers and from the hedgerow trees come the calls of nestlings pleading to be fed. Enjoy the richness of the vegetation before you begin your trek of the treeless Howgills.

As you go you pass first, on the left, the entrance to Whins Farm. Beyond, go on along the lane to the access track, on the left, to Beck House farm-

Nestlings in the hedge - young bluetits

house, signposted 'Footpath to Black Force'. A concrete track leads to the pretty farmhouse, where you keep to the right of the dwelling. Pass through two gates and walk

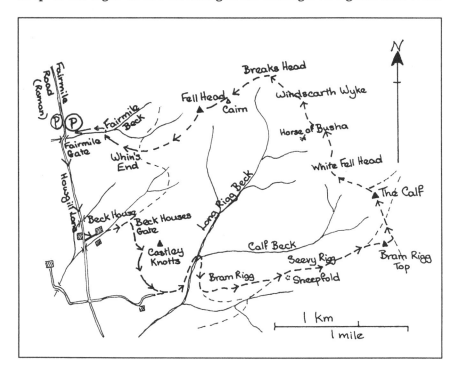

on a few metres to come beside the remnants of an old building on your left. Drop down to the beck on your right and step across at a convenient spot.

Continue in the same general direction, walking the right edge of an old sunken lane which brings you to a sheepfold at Beck Houses Gate (two and sometimes three gates). Beyond, turn right and follow the grassy path, just above the wall. Where the wall turns down right, go on ahead on the same contour, winding round the skirt of Castley Knotts. On reaching the wall again, at a corner, descend the slope with it to your right to join the bridleway from Castley (walk 15).

Turn left and walk the wide track below the east side of the Knotts as it steadily descends to a ford over Long Rigg Beck. There is a row of boulders on which to cross when the beck is quite low. From here look left and up on the slopes of Bush Howe to see the 'horse of busha', a natural phenomenon of stones which have fallen into the shape of a horse, with a grassy patch in just the right place for an eye.

Beyond the beck, turn right to cross Calf Beck and follow wheel-marks up the slope. Then at the highest point, head left to follow sheep trods or wheelmarks to Sevy Rigg 1181ft (360m).

A footpath leads to a largish sheepfold, and beyond a fine, wide track continues steadily upwards. After a good climb the way

The Horse of Busha

divides, one path leading along the side of Bram Rigg, (care is needed in two places) the other continuing to the top, 2205ft (672m). From here you have a spectacular view of Fell End Clouds – if the sun is shining the limestone appears a brilliant white.

Whichever route you have taken, join a wide track and walk left, gently uphill to the trig point on The Calf. At 2218ft (676m) and the highest point in the Howgills, the view is magnificent.

Stand by the trig point with your back to your approach path and look for the glorious ridge path stretching ahead (north) over the fells. (The other good path leads off east towards Bowderdale.)

Stride the glorious path as it by-passes White Fell. Look right to see a long, wide part of Langdale enclosed by steep-sided fells. The path goes on to the Height of Bush Howe and then Bush Howe. Then comes the unexpected descent to Windscarth Wyke, an exciting saddle with the fell dropping away on both sides. The way continues straight up a steep slope to Breaks Head, 2093ft (638m) and then curves left (west).

Stroll the pleasing ridge path. Look for the Screes of Black Force, Uldale Head, Uldale and Hand Lake (walks 19 and 32). The summit has a small cairn, 2100ft (640m). Carry on towards Fell Head, 2044ft (623m), on the continuing good path. This cairn lies to the right of the path and, after visiting the pile of stones, return to the path so that you can go on down the steepish slope. If you miss the start of this path, the descent has to be made over the rough fell grass.

The distinct but narrow way goes down and down to join the bridle path to Black Force – not very clear at this point. Ignore this track and stroll on in the same general direction along the spine of Whin's End, 1260ft (384m). Pause at the highest part and, before you descend, look half right to see your parked vehicle and also the wall corner beside Fairmile Beck. Then make a beeline for the beck, over the pathless fell. Descend to the beck at the best place and either head downstream to reach Fairmile Road, or clamber out of the gill and stride across the pasture to rejoin your car.

Walk 19: Gibbet Hill – Linghaw – Uldale Head

Carlingill Bridge – Gibbet Hill – Back Balk – Linghaw – Little Ulgill Head – Blakethwaite Bottom – Uldale Head – Weasel Gill – Gibbet Hill

Start/finish: On the side of Fairmile Road, Gibbet Hill (GR 625995). If approaching from the M6, leave by the Tebay junction and at the roundabout turn into Tebay village. Re-cross the M6 and take the next left turn, signposted Sedbergh, to pass under the motorway and the railway viaduct. Follow the narrow road (which has some passing places) to cross Carlingill Bridge, and park at the top of the slope.

Type of walk: An exciting 4½ miler. Tractor paths take you easily to the top of Linghaw, which appears so forbidding from Gibbet Hill. A narrow path winds round the top of a great cleft and then continues above the ravine of Carlin Beck, bringing you to the remote hollow of Blakethwaite Bottom. The way up to Uldale Head again follows a tractor route. From there on the way is pathless until you find the grooved track, an old drove road, that descends to Carlin Beck.

Map: OS Outdoor Leisure 19 Howgill Fells and Upper Eden Valley

---

The Walk

Gibbet Hill is said to be the place where sheep stealers were hanged. It lies on Fairmile Road, built over a stretch of the Roman road along which supplies would have been carried to the Roman camp at Borrow Bridge. The hill ascends, south, from Carlingill Bridge, once a packhorse route over Carlin Beck. Here the stream hurries through

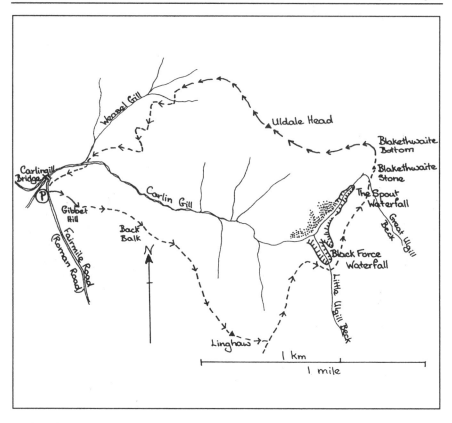

a delightful tree-lined ravine. It is the haunt of grey wagtails, and in summer you might see sand martins catching insects riskily sunbathing on the narrow road.

Leave the road from the corner, above the bridge, by a narrow path and begin to climb the slopes. The path gradually bears right, away from Carlin Gill which lies to your left. Then the upward way continues as a wide grassy track made by tractor wheels. As you go (in summer) watch out for shy fell ponies with their foals.

When the tractor way ceases and a slope rears up more steeply, go on up a 'stepped' path. This joins another distinct path, where you turn left and continue to the cairnless summit of Linghaw, 1640ft (500m). From here you can see the wide Lune valley and Killington Lake, the Scafells and Gable beyond the motorway.

Descend steadily to a crossroads of paths on the saddle, between Linghaw and Fell Head, to join the old sheep path from Howgill Lane. Turn left. The fine, narrow path is edged with pale mauve violets in summer and curves gracefully round the edge of Blake Ridge. Now you can enjoy a bird's eye view of Carlin Gill far below, but as the fell drops away steeply to your left, it would be wiser to stop

Rock formation above Black Spout

while you do so. Pause also to look ahead for your first view of The Spout, the dramatic waterfall on the Carlin where it drops into the head of the gill.

Then the good path briefly disappears. Go on around a curve in the fell and before you a wide grassy track descends to the side of Little Ulgill Beck, just before it begins its tumultuous descent as Black Force.

Step across the mountain stream and walk on for a dozen paces. Look back at the near-perpendicular strata of rock in the enormous cleft. Here rowans cling precariously. Go on with care along the narrow path, with an ever improving view of The Spout. And then the path descends easily to Great Ulgill Beck and Blakethwaite Bottom (walk 32).

Follow the path, where the lowly New Zealand willowherb flourishes in the crevice of a fractured rock, its little pink flowers thrusting skywards. Cross the grassy hollow to the boundary stone (walk 32). To your right is Over Sail, ahead Docker Knott and to its left Hand Lake (walk 32). Be vigilant here, for you might see a peregrine circling on the thermals. Its nest is probably a rough hollow scraped on a ledge, high above Black Force.

Turn left and begin your ascent of Uldale Head. There is a narrow path and this joins a tractor route as you climb. Before reaching the summit, and if you wish to see Black Force, head off left and peer with great care.

To continue, go on along the clear way to the summit's small cairn, 1739ft (530m). The view from the top is magnificent. Look for Morecambe Bay and Arnside Knott, the Pennines and many of the Lakeland tops.

Follow the clear grassy way to another small cairn. Then go on along the continuing tractor path for a short distance until you reach a pool to your left, below a line of peat hags. Once past the pool swing left, west, and walk over the featureless fell in the direction of the re-

Peregrine

peater station high on Whinfell Beacon on the far side of the motorway. It stands out clearly across the pastures.

Look for a grooved track, once a drove road, that descends in a huge zig-zag, bringing you safely to the valley bottom. There are several grooves, made presumably by large herds of cattle. Today they are filled with rushes. Walk the edge of one of the grooves, choosing the easiest route.

Cross a small feeder stream that joins Weasel Gill and continue down, through bracken, to come to the side of Carlin Beck. If the beck is low, cross as the cattle did and go on the continuing path to rejoin your car. If the beck is impassable, cross Weasel Gill in the valley bottom and follow a sheep trod above the Carlin to pass through a gate by Carlingill Bridge.

Walk 20: Blease Fell and Hare Shaw

Old Tebay – Mount Pleasant – Tebay Gill – Powson Knott –
Blease Fell – Hare Shaw – Knott – Gill Hole – Gaisgill –
Rayne Bridge – Raisgill Hall – Coatflatt Hall – Tebay Bridge
– River Lune – Old Tebay

Start/finish: A lay-by in Old Tebay by the footpath leading to the River Lune (GR 617052). The lay-by is on the B6260, 2½ miles south of Orton. The long, rambling village of Tebay lies midway between Penrith in the north and Kendal in the south, close to where the Birk Beck joins the River Lune. Tebay is situated just off the M6, which you leave at junction 38.

Type of walk: Save this challenging 9-mile route of contrasting terrain and glorious views for a fine day. For much of the fell walking there are reinforced tracks and grassy trods to help you on your way – there is also an area of peat hags to be skirted. The return route takes you on paths just above the River Lune, visiting the site of a cockpit. This part of the walk is generally well signposted and most of its stiles are in good repair and can be attempted whatever the weather.

Map: OS Outdoor Leisure 19 Howgill Fells and Upper Eden Valley

---

The Walk

Leave the lay-by in Old Tebay and walk south along the road, which is lined with cottages. These overlook, to the east, the defunct railway link (North Eastern Railway) between Darlington and the main (west) line to Scotland. The 'new' A685 has been built over the route of the old line from Tebay to Newbiggin-on-Lune, leaving the hamlets that cluster the old A-road in peace.

Cross the roundabout with care, and continue ahead towards Tebay. Where the road bears right, and just before a toilet block, turn left into the old A685 and walk ahead. A few paces along, on your right, is the old school which was endowed by Robert Adamson in 1672. It has been converted into a county venture hostel.

Turn right just beyond the old school to walk a metalled track leading towards the fells. Cross the cattle grid and at a Y-junction take the right fork. At the next Y-junction, again take the right branch. Then at the next division of the ways, leave the metalled track and take the left fork. Continue ahead, gently ascending, to pass Tebaygill Farm and then a small barn.

Pass through a gate in the fence and at the next Y-junction take the right branch, with a fence to your right. To the far right is a grand view of the Lakeland Fells beyond the M6. Now you are up among the meadow pipits; in spring the air resounds with their songs. Where the fence turns away right, go on along the green track, at first indistinct but soon becoming clearer. Pause here to look down, right, on the charming hamlet of Roundthwaite.

Meadow pipit

Where the green track ends go on upwards on a narrow path, keeping either right or left of Powson Knott, a grassy knoll, 1227ft (374m). Beyond, a grassy trod continues and passes a group of small, peaty pools on your left. To your left you can look into Tebay Gill and beyond it Hare Shaw. Ahead is Blease Fell, 1555ft (474m), and towards this you continue, with little evidence of a path. Pause regularly to enjoy the wonderful views.

Go on through a wettish area and then onto the summit and, just beyond, to a sturdy cairn. Where did all the stones come from in this area of rolling moorland which has no walls or outcrops of rock? Ahead you can look into Carlin Gill. To your right the vehicles on the M6, where it passes through the Lune gorge, appear like dozens of multicoloured ants scurrying in opposing directions. In the far distance you can spot the Duddon estuary and the submarine shed at Barrow.

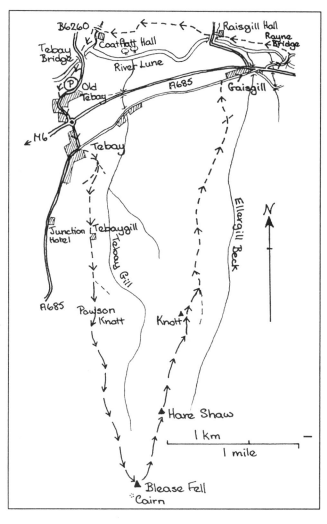

From the cairn swing left to continue to Hare Shaw, seen earlier across Tebay Gill. Keep well to the right of a large area of peat hags, but not too far right to lose height. Continue bearing left to join the tractor tracks, which ascend gently to the cairn on the summit, 1549ft (472m). From here you can see, to your left, the Coniston range of hills stretching away to Black Combe, and the High Street range. Ahead is a vast panorama of the Pennine hills, where Cross Fell will probably have its head in the clouds.

Leave the summit and descend easily, now with Tebay Gill to your left and Eller Gill to your right. Continue to the next grassy top, Knott, 1283ft (391m), and continue edging over to the right to pick up a good farm track. At this point, look across Ellergill Beck to see the picturesque remains of Raw Busk Farm.

Soon the track comes beside a wall, a pleasure to see after so much featureless fell. Ahead is a glorious patchwork of walls, hedgerows and copses around the pastures about the River Lune. Away to your left is the Blue Marble quarry on Shap and you can also see the tower of Orton church. Look out for the shy, glossy black fell ponies, which you are asked not to feed. Go on where the track becomes tarmacked and at the T-junction, turn right to pass under scots pine, ash and lime into the hamlet of Gaisgill. Notice the cottages and their datestones.

Keep on the narrow, former A-road to pass on your right the small Wesleyan chapel (1841), now a Methodist church. Look for the memorial stones set into the wall. On your left is the old reading room, dated 1909. Go on to the busy 'new' road. Fifty metres along on the right, take the left turn (the old A-road) and continue to cross Langdale Beck and then on to Rayne Bridge over the Lune. From this bridge Thomas Bowness-Wright, a schoolmaster of Langdale school, liked to watch otters playing in the lovely river. He recorded his observations in letters to his friend, who had them published after Thomas's death. The book, now out of print, is entitled *The Watcher by the Bridge.*

At the far left side of the parapet, squeeze through a very narrow gap stile to descend steps. Stride straight up the slope and follow a grooved way which bears left (downstream). Pass through a stile in the wall from where there is a fine view of the valley below and the area where you walked earlier. Go on the gap-stiled way. The path continues in the same general direction on the slopes above the river. The stiles, which are set in the boundary walls, are often difficult to spot but lie approximately opposite the one taken previously.

Climb the stile before Raisgill Hall. The circular depression in front of you is an old cockpit. Cock-fighting, a popular and ancient sport, was made illegal in 1835. Cocks were fitted with steel cockspurs over the top of their natural spurs. The soil thrown up during the digging of the cockpit formed a circular wall over which the spectators could lean to watch the fighting.

Bear right below the pit. Follow the arrows to the Orton road. Turn left, walk 50 metres and then cross the road to pass through a signposted gate. Climb the steepish slope and go through another gate. Turn right and follow the wall, on your right, all the way to an arrowed gate, through which you pass. Continue on in the same general direction to pass through another gate, with the wall to your left. Saunter past a small planting of sycamores on your left to go through a gate into a walled area. Follow the grassy way as it bears left. Pass a pool to your right and continue diagonally across a walled pasture, towards some trees. Go through the gap and continue with a wall to the right and descend towards a grassy track leading to the dwellings at Coatflatt Hall.

Follow the track as it swings sharp right to pass behind barns and a house to go through a gate. Bear left to cross Chapel Beck on a tractor bridge. Stride ahead. Ignore the access track climbing the slope and swing left to walk beside the beck to a gap stile in the wall ahead. Continue on the raised bank of a small ditch. Cross the beck on large slabs and go on to Tebay Bridge.

A stone-stepped stile leads up to the Orton road. Turn left, cross the bridge and take the signposted path on the right. Stroll on beside the wide river. Just before the M6, look for the track going off left. This leads you back to the lay-by where you have parked.

Walk 21: Orton – Gaythorne Plain – Robin Hood's Grave

Orton – Broadfell Farm – Street Lane – Scar Side Farm – Gaythorne Plain – Bank Farm – Holme Bridge – Crosby Lodge Farm – Robin Hood's Grave – Orton

Start/finish: Parking area in the square in the centre of Orton (GR 623083)

Type of walk: Orton is a delightful village from which to start this 9½ miler. It is situated in the northern part of what was once Westmorland, on the Appleby to Kendal road. The picturesque houses and cottages surround the 13th-century church. Its tower, which can be seen from the outlying parts of the village, dates from the early 16th century. The village lies at the foot of Orton Scar. In early spring the shy golden plover nests on coarse grass between the limestone boulders and fills the air with its plaintive piping. This long walk continues almost to Crosby Ravensworth and then returns beside the lovely Lyvennet Beck. It goes on over the pastures of Hollins Scar, continues past Robin Hood's grave and then goes on through glorious heather, magnificent in August. There is some rough walking over Gaythorne Plain, but otherwise this is a delightful country stroll.

Map: OS Outdoor Leisure 19 Howgill Fells and Upper Eden Valley

The Walk

Walk north along the Appleby road from the parking area and take the first right turn. Continue past the Old Vicarage, on your left, and then take the next left turn, a 'no through road'. Walk the quiet lane

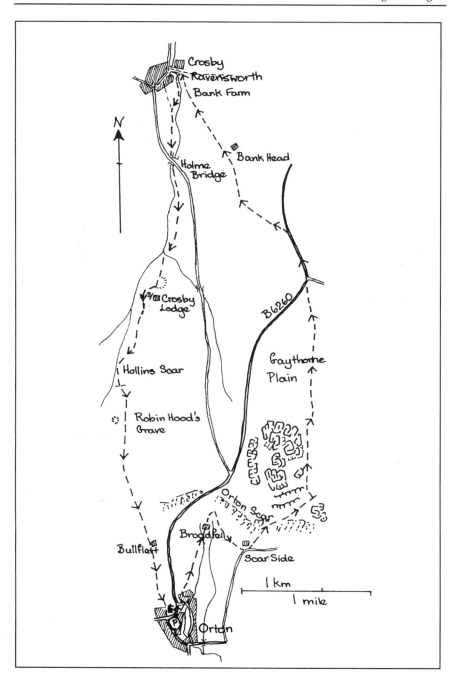

and leave it at the first signpost, a left turn, for Broadfell. The way winds right, crosses a trim lawn and then continues along a narrow path between hedgerows. Go on to a stile, beyond which lie the flower-bedecked banks of the beck.

Golden plovers

Cross the footbridge and then head across the gated pasture to the left side of Broadfell Farm. Go through more gates in the farmyard and continue beside the wall on your left to a gate to the fell. Do not pass through but bear right to cross a footbridge and go on with a wall to your left to join the access track from Broadfell.

At the track end, walk left along Street Lane. Pass Scar Side Farm, where the lane swings right. Go on to take the stile on the left before a gate over the lane. Walk ahead to a stile to the right of a gate. Beyond, stride on with the wall to your left and press on over two haymeadows on the same diagonal to pass through a gate in the fell wall.

Bear right and walk to a wall gap. Beyond, join a tractor track as it steadily climbs the slope to the boundary wall ahead. Stay beside the wall, now on your right, to a gap onto open limestone fell. Continue straight up the fell to pass through an ornate gate. Beyond, pause to get your bearings. Look left to see Beacon Hill and its monument, a mock Celtic cross installed in 1887. Look right to see, stretching away right, the continuing boundary wall. The route of the walk continues ahead between these two landmarks. In parts there is a good track. In many places there is just a sheep trod, and in some nothing to guide you except keeping north over Gaythorne Plain.

Once you can see vehicles on the Appleby road, away to your left, keep parallel with them. The track, so good on the OS map and so indistinct on the ground, brings you, after a mile-and-a half from the gate, to the junction of the Appleby and Great Asby roads. Join the main road and walk on, using the grass verge, to a footpath sign on the brow of the hill. From here you can see Dufton and Cross Fell. The wide grassy path leads off left and, after the sometimes rough passage over the Plain, is a joy to walk.

The way becomes metalled and pleasantly hedged, and soon Crosby Ravensworth comes into view, nestling among pastures. Pass Bank Farm and continue on the lane if you wish to visit the village. To go on with the walk, look for the grassy ride going off left just beyond Bank Farm, and leading to a footbridge over the Lyvennet Beck, which you cross. Take the stile on the left and walk with the tree-shaded beck to your left. Follow the well-signposted way, which has easy stiles. Continue to Holme Bridge.

Cross the bridge and take the signposted way in the direction of Orton, with the beck now to your right. Stride the stiled way. After crossing what is in effect the last wooden stile and on reaching a wall, walk uphill beside the wall to find the stile just beyond a gate. Go on and when you reach an access track to Crosby Lodge, join it and go downhill (bearing right) to cross a hollow near the beck. Proceed up the track to Crosby Lodge.

Pass a bank barn and then go through double gates. Turn right immediately and walk to the right of outbuildings. Bear round left to go through another gate. Stride on, skirting the outside wall of the farm, to join a track. Walk on to pass through the next gate to where the track divides. Take the right branch to go through scattered hawthorns which cover the slope that drops to the beck.

Ignore the gate in the wall corner on your left and also the step stile in the wall just beyond. Pass through the next gate, further along the same wall, on your left and walk right (in the same general direction) to the rim of a grassy gill that stretches ahead. Descend to the foot of the gill to pass a conical pile of stones, named as Robin Hood's grave on the OS map. Keep straight ahead and then on the continuing narrow path through, in August and September, colour-

Robin Hood's Grave

ful, sweet-smelling heather to a prominent ladder stile. Beyond, the footpath continues to Orton, the stiles, gates and gateposts being marked with white paint. The final stile leads you to Orton's All Saints Church. Go inside and look for the parish chest and the old bread charity chest. From the church a short wide track leads quickly to the centre of the village.

Walk 22: Orton – Great Asby

Knott Lane – Asby Scar – Sayle Lane – Great Asby – Town
Head – Sunbiggin – Knott Lane

Start/finish: Knott Lane, a wide grassy track which leads to
                      Orton Scar (GR 639079). Please avoid parking in
                      front of all gates and stiles. The track lies a mile
                      east of Orton on the Raisbeck Road.

Type of walk: An extensive area of limestone, Great Asby Scar,
                      is crossed twice on this glorious 9-miler. Huge
                      stretches of clints, with tiny gardens of ferns and
                      other lowly plants nestling in the grykes, turn
                      these heights into a weird, lonely landscape and a
                      delectable place for a walk.

Map: OS Outdoor Leisure 19 Howgill Fells and Upper
                      Eden Valley

The Walk

Continue along the walled Knott Lane, which leads towards Orton
Scar. Look over the wall on the right to
see a circle of 24 stones. Just before the
fell gate stands a sturdy limekiln built of
large blocks of stone.

Beyond the gate, follow the clear track
that bears slightly left, continuing uphill
beside a splendid limestone wall, into
the territory of the skylark, meadow
pipit and wheatear. Enjoy the pleasing
view of the attractive village of Orton
lying at the foot of its Scar, its houses
gathered around its parish church of All
Saints.

Wheatear

Great Asby Scar

Pass through the gate in the wall ahead and bear half right, keeping below a dramatic limestone ridge, now on your left. The grassy way soon becomes clear and, after a pleasing stroll, you come to a stile in the wall into the nature reserve.

A board welcomes you to Asby Scar. It says this is one of the best developed examples of pavement and that it was laid down when the area was a shallow, warm sea. After millions of years the limestone was uplifted and buckled, the surface pattern being created by glacial action. You are reminded to walk with care over the clints and grykes, especially after wet weather.

Walk ahead from the stile and then follow an easy-to-miss grassy way, which goes on bearing right to pass through the dramatic rock formations to another notice board and a gate out of the reserve. Cut across the corner of the pasture to a gate. Beyond, walk ahead with a wall to the right and go on along the continuing walled track to pass below Andrew Scar. This joins Sayle Lane, a quiet metalled way which passes, in spring, through pastures full of sheep and lambs. It descends into Great Asby, the name meaning 'where ash trees grow'.

This picturesque village stretches along either side of Ash Beck. It is often dry and flows only after heavy rain fills the kettle holes higher up. The beck is crossed by several bridges and it is pleasant

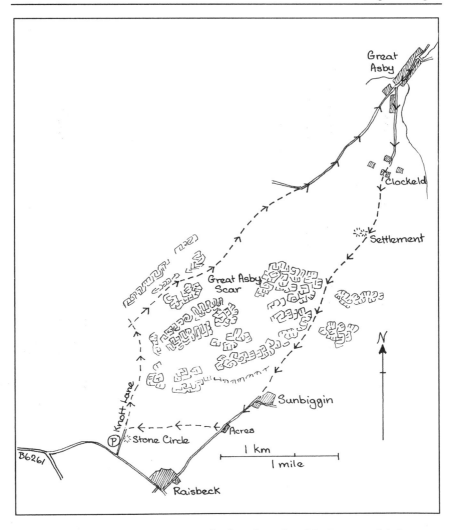

to walk along either side towards the church of St Peter, which soon dominates your view. Opposite the church is The Three Greyhounds public house, with its stone dogs sitting on the wall. Further on stands Asby Hall, built in 1694 and once the home of the powerful Musgrave family, whose arms are displayed above the door.

Return past the church and walk beside Well Green, where a spring gushes forth (St Helen's Well). It is reputed never to freeze or dry up, and below it the beck has water. Close by is St Helen's almshouse, built in the early 19th century. Continue on (south) past the attractive 17th and 18th-century cottages to take the 'no through road' to the left of the road to Orton down which you walked earlier.

Climb the lane, which is colourful with wild flowers in spring, to pass through Town Head. At the end of the metalled way, go on through a waymarked metal gate to walk to the right of Clockeld farmhouse. Continue ahead to follow the excellently waymarked bridleway, where no instructions are needed. In May and June listen as you go for the calls of nesting curlews and green plovers.

At the three-armed signpost, walk in the direction of Sunbiggin and Sunbiggin Tarn. Look right to see turf banks enclosing humps and hollows, all part of an ancient settlement. Press on along the well-waymarked route, with High Pike to your right. After a vast area of pavement the bridleway begins its steady descent to the road at the hamlet of Sunbiggin. Turn right and walk the narrow lane to the next dwelling, named Acres.

Pass through the double gate opposite and strike left. From here a stiled way continues over the pastures, keeping to the right of the first barn you can see and then to the left of the next. This well-maintained way leads you to Knott Lane via the pasture above the stone circle. Turn left to rejoin your car.

Walk 23: Crosby Garrett – Potts valley

Crosby Garrett – Ladle Lane (track) – Wander Bank – Potts Farm – Groups Hollows – Potts Valley – Fell Head – Ewefell Mire – Bents – Beacon Hill – Crosby Garrett

Start/finish:	Crosby Garrett (GR 729095). The village lies 4 miles from Kirkby Stephen and 7 miles from Appleby-in-Westmorland. Park in one of several lay-bys beside the beck in the centre of the village.
Type of walk:	A delightful 7½ miler through wonderful, quiet countryside. The path beside Potts Beck, with limestone outcropping on either side, is a joy. Easy walking all the way.
Map:	OS Outdoor Leisure 19 Howgill Fells and the Upper Eden Valley

The Walk

Pleasing houses and cottages line the narrow Crosby Garrett Beck, which flows through the village. Dominating one end of the village is the 54 foot (16m) viaduct of the Settle-Carlisle railway. At the northern end, on the highest part of the ridge known as Arklow, stands the parish church of St Andrew. On top of this mound pre-Christian sacrifices are thought to have been made.

Walk the road in the direction of the church and continue with it high on your right. Take an unsignposted left turn to walk in front of an old building with the datemark 1714 above its door. Continue on a green track towards a bungalow and turn left to walk a narrow, hedged track. At a narrow road, turn right and continue uphill, ignoring the footpath on the left. Go on to the end of the tarmac and then swing left to cross a railway bridge.

Just beyond, bear left to follow Ladle Lane as it swings right. It climbs steadily, first between flower-filled hedgerows and then

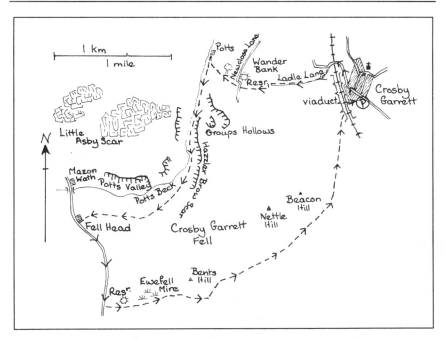

walled pastures, with the shapely silhouette of Wild Boar Fell (walk 5) coming into view on your left and the Pennines on your right. Pass a fine bank barn on the right. Continue on to where the track makes a sharp left turn – and it is often very muddy – to go ahead through an unsignposted gate. Continue along a wide track, with walled pastures stretching away to the left and a grass-sided small reservoir above on Wander Bank. Go through a gate to cross Newclose Lane (a track).

Stroll ahead, with the wall to your left, until you reach some scattered hawthorns. Just beyond, take the stile over the wall on your left, before the boundary wall ahead. Stride steadily downhill (with the wall, heavily encrusted with lichen, now on your right) to a gate. Pass through and follow the track, right, to the side of sadly deserted Potts Farm, set in an idyllic hollow.

Turn left and follow the clear path upstream beside Potts Beck on your right, here edged with ash and hawthorn. Ahead are the eastern slopes of Little Asby Scar. Go on the stiled way beside the dancing, pellucid beck. Now the slopes to the left are littered with limestone boulders. Stroll on through Groups Hollows to pass below, on the left, Hazzler Brow Scar.

Follow the grassy trod as it moves away from the beck across the lower slopes of Crosby Garrett Fell, passing several water board hydrant posts. At hydrant number 10, take the narrow trod climbing towards the corner of several walled pastures – one has a barn in it with a chimney. (Ignore the large, walled sheepfold high up on the left.)

Potts Beck

Walk beside the wall and barn, now on your right, and, where the wall turns away right, go ahead on the wide grassy trod over the heather moorland. The track joins the road above Fell Head, an attractive white dwelling with green doors. Below, close to Potts Beck, is the farm of Mazon Wath. Turn left and ascend the fell road through more heather moorland. Cross the cattle grid and go on with an extensive view of the Howgills. Immediately ahead is the fell Green Bell (walk 29).

Take the reinforced track going off left, towards another small, grass-sided reservoir and then continue beside the wall on your right. Pass Ewefell Mire and go through a gate to the left of a barn. Beyond, three tracks stretch ahead. Take the grassy one on the right and continue parallel with the friendly wall, still to your right, to come to the signpost at Bents, and a section of Wainwright's Coast to Coast (CC) walk.

Go on again with the wall to your right. Ignore the gate in the wall, through which the CC continues, and remain beside the wall, climbing a small slope. And then the glorious high-level way goes on and on, with Nettle Hill and Beacon Hill to your left and glorious views across Smardale Gill (walk 24) to your right.

The track becomes reinforced where you joined it on walk 24 and begins its descent towards Crosby Garrett, with the upper Eden valley stretched out before you. As you near the village look for a limekiln on the right, and then pass under the viaduct to rejoin your car.

Walk 24: Smardale Gill – Crosby Garrett

Beck Lane, Smardale – Smardale Gill – Viaduct – Limekilns –
Crosby Garrett – Beck Lane

Start/finish: A small parking area on the left of the private
access road to Smardale Hall (GR 739083). The
access road is a narrow turning off south from the
narrow Beck Lane. The parking area is the yard of
the former Smardale Station on the disused South
Durham and Lancashire Union Railway. After rain
the ford over the Scandal Beck might be trouble-
some so it is better to approach from Kirkby
Stephen, which lies 3 miles to the east.

Type of walk: Woodland, rough fell, quiet pastures and riverside
paths make this a delightful 6-mile walk.

Map: OS Outdoor Leisure 19 Howgill Fells and Upper
Eden Valley

The Walk

From the parking area, climb the slope opposite to join the old
railway track managed by Cumbria Wildlife Trust. Parts of the gill
were acquired by the trust in 1978. Since then they have bought
more land and now own more than 40 hectares (100 acres). Walk on
the glorious way.

Smardale Gill was chosen by Thomas Bouch, the engineer of the
South Durham and Lancashire Union railway, as the preferred route
between Kirkby Stephen on the River Eden and Tebay on the River
Lune. The railway was needed to transport coke from County
Durham to smelt the haematite iron ore which occurred in the
Furness area of Lancashire. Its construction made possible the
establishment of shipbuilding at Barrow, in what was known as the
iron-clad era.

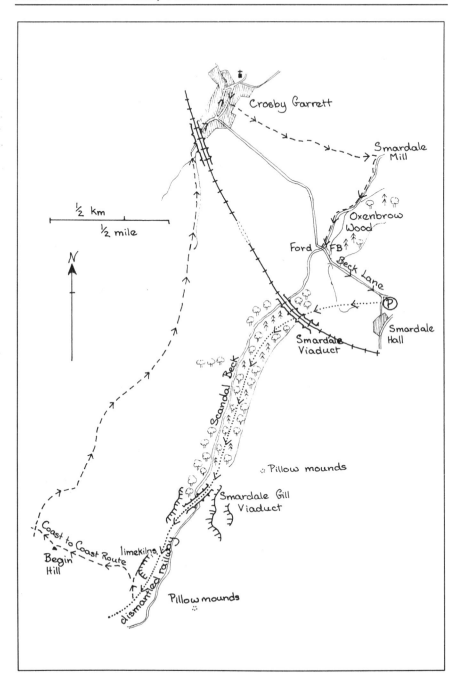

Continue through the pleasing woodland, which in spring is full of birdsong and carpeted with celandines, wood anemone and wood sorrel. Look left for a glimpse of Smardale Hall, a 13th-century fortified hall, now a farmhouse. It is a long, rectangular building with round towers at its four corners.

Stroll on to pass under the Smardale viaduct. It is 130ft (40m) high and

Celandines and wood anemones

has 12 arches It carries the Settle and Carlisle railway and is regularly used. Beyond, look down, right, on Scandal Beck which, rising on Mallerstang Common, has cut a deep gill through the carboniferous limestone, forming the steep-sided gorge.

Emerge from the trees to cross Smardale Gill viaduct, which lies obliquely across the gill. It is 90ft (27m) high and stretches for 500ft (152m) across its 14 flaring arches. In 1987 it qualified for an English Heritage grant. It is a magnificent construction and the views from it are dramatic.

Saunter along the track to pass two large limekilns. These provided the mortar required for building both viaducts. Pause at a small footbridge and look across the gill to see several oblong grassy mounds, called pillar mounds on the OS map. No one quite knows their purpose; some think they are artificial warrrens for rabbits, others that they might have been used for drying bracken.

Walk on to pass two derelict houses and then go under a bridge over the track. Take a stile on the left immediately beyond. Then turn left to join the Coast to Coast walk (CC) and cross over the bridge. Follow the arrows directing you right to avoid tramping across the ancient settlement of Severals. At the wall turn left and climb up beside it, staying beside it as it swings to the left over Begin Hill. Pass through a well signposted stile in the wall.

At this point you leave the CC walk and go on a narrow grassy path, keeping to the right of the overhead power lines. These take you safely over an extensive, rather featureless pasture to come to a

Smardale Gill Viaduct

gate in the wall ahead (noted on walk 23). Beyond, join a wide, reinforced track to walk right. This takes you steadily downhill to pass under a 54ft (16m) high viaduct on the Settle-Carlisle railway into the attractive village of Crosby Garrett.

Walk on through the village, which is intersected by Crosby Garrett Beck. This is crossed by small clapper bridges. Ahead stands the church of St Andrew on its mound. To visit obtain the key from the vicarage beyond the church.

Return a short way through the village, keeping to the east (left side) of the beck, to take the gap stile on the left, signposted Smardale Mill. Walk ahead through buildings and then along a grassy way. Pass through the gate and walk ahead across a pasture to a gate in the far left corner to join a hedged track. Pass through the next gate and walk on. Look for the gate on the right, which gives access to another hedged track, where you turn left.

Walk the pleasing way as it gradually descends to a footbridge over the Scandal Beck. Do not cross but take the stile on the right to continue beside the lovely stream. Across the river is Oxenbrow Wood, where herons nest. Stroll on to come to Tarn Lane, where you turn left, using the footbridge beyond the ford. Carry on along what is now called Beck Lane to return to the parking area on the right.

Walk 25: Kirkby Stephen – Soulby

Kirkby Stephen – Waitby – Waitby Crossing – Scandal Beck
– Soulby – River Eden – Winton – Hartley Fold – Kirkby
Stephen

Start/finish: Free car park by Kirkby Stephen School, north-
west end of the town (GR 774088).

Type of walk: This pleasant 8½ miler visits the hamlets and vil-
lages of Waitby, Soulby, Winton and Hartley Fold,
using hedged green lanes, footpaths, byways (de-
scribed by the OS map as open to all traffic) and
some roads. The road walking is unavoidable because of the dearth of footpaths, but most roads
are narrow and have grass growing along the middle, and you are likely to meet only farm vehicles.
This makes a good winter walk when the tops are
veiled in mist or when the wind makes them inhos-
pitable. In spring and early summer the hedges
resound to the songs of migrants, and throughout
the summer the hedgerows are ablaze with wild
flowers. Autumn brings the hips, haws, sloes and
nuts and all the lovely colours of the ageing vegetation.

Map: OS Outdoor Leisure 19 Howgill Fells and Upper
Eden Valley

The Walk

Return to the road from the car park and turn left to walk beside the
school to a Y-junction. Ignore both roads and take the green lane on
the left, signposted Galebars and Greenriggs. Walk the delightful
way, with Stobars Hall across pastures on the right.

After 300 metres, where the track divides, take the right branch

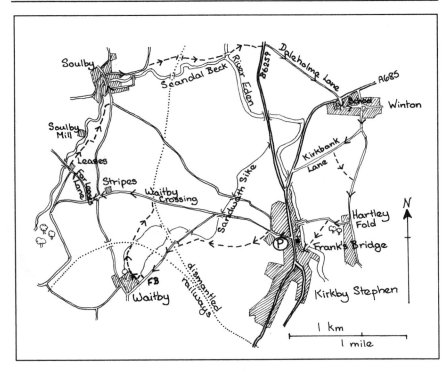

to walk to a clearly waymarked stile. Go ahead beside the hedge on your right and then descend the continuing gated track to its end.

Pass through the gate on your right, leave the track to the farm and bear left across the grass to a tractor bridge over Sandwath Syke. Cross the pasture and take the waymarked tractor bridge on your right. Go on ahead to the next gate, and before it turn left to walk beside the hedge on your right. Stride to a gap stile in the corner ahead. Pass through and turn right to stroll to another very narrow gap stile to a lane.

Turn left and climb the quiet way, where in late May the verges are a mass of water avens, cowslips, violets, wild arum and Jack-by-the-hedge. Cross the bridge over the disused railway line that once ran towards Appleby and Penrith and stroll on to cross another – the continuation of the line that passes through Smardale Gill (walk 24).

Here you might wish to make a diversion to enjoy the Cumbria

Wildlife Trust's small nature reserve. A map is displayed on a board. The route takes you south-east along this disused track to the junction with the other. In the sheltered environment provided by the steep banks, cowslips grow in great profusion.

Stroll on for 510 metres to take, on the right, a track, the signpost obscured by vegetation in the summer. Follow the hedged way over the Waitby Beck, a tiny stream, and then climb up the slope to pass between the dwellings of the hamlet. It is thought that Waitby was once a market town with a chapel, cemetery and castle, but there is no trace of these now. A school on Waitby Fell for the children of Smardale and Waitby was closed in 1930.

Head for the telephone box and then take the signposted byway for Waitby Crossing. The route is along

Cowslips

a reinforced track which passes between the embankments, once bridged, of the old railway. Beyond, turn right and after 90 metres ignore the stile on the left, as well as the track which bears off right, and go on along the lovely lane. Follow it as it swings left and comes to the crossing house. Turn left to stride another very quiet lane, with grass growing along its crown.

Stroll on past a house called Stripes, which has its doors and windows painted blue. At the tiny crossroads carry on ahead to take the first turning on the right – an even narrower lane, its banks colourful with flowers, and it, too, with grass along its middle.

Pass a house called Leases and take the signposted gate on the right. Walk right, with the house to your right and the Scandal Beck, across the meadow, to your left. Go through a sturdy gate into a flower-filled copse beside the beck. Follow the narrow path and then leave the trees by a gate on your right. Stride on along the river bank to the next stile, also on your right. Pause here to look across the beck to Soulby Mill, closed in the 1950s. Here on a reach of pebbles, in summer, oysters catchers nest and call noisily when disturbed by passers-by.

Beyond the stile mentioned above, the way differs from the OS map. Walk beside the fence on the left and go with it as it turns left – watching out for stock (see below). Keep to the left side of the pasture, well away from two duck ponds. At the end of the fence pass through a gate in the right corner to walk a track with a copse to your left. The track can be very muddy after rain as it is used by cattle. Pass through the next gate and strike right across the pasture to a gate to the road junction.

The pastures referred to above are used by a farmer who keeps several bulls. If you need an escape route, having climbed the stile and entered the pasture, continue on to join a track ahead which services the duck ponds. Pass through a very awkward gate and go on to the road. Turn left and walk to the road junction. At this point the escape route and the way over the pasture meet up. Walk on into Soulby.

This delightful village stands on the banks of Scandal Beck, which is spanned by a sturdy three-arched bridge. The beck bisects the spacious village green, in the north-west corner of which stands the village pump in an ivy-clad enclosure. It was erected in 1888 and until 1938 supplied most of the residents of the village with their drinking water.

Cross the bridge. To continue the walk you will need to take the second turning on the right, signposted Great and Little Musgrave.

But before you go on you may wish to visit the quaint church, St Luke's, which you can see ahead on the left. It was built by Sir Philip Musgrave of Hartley Castle in 1662. In 1874 it was extensively repaired and adorned. Look for the interesting plaque over the church door and the fine weather vane.

Weather vane

If you have visited the church, take the signposted turn now on your left and stride the lane to pass the cemetery on your left. Ignore the footpath on the right and continue for 45 metres to take, on the right, the public byway to Winton. Cross the disused railway line and stroll on to where the track divides. Take the left branch. In summer, the track is edged by the aromatic sweet cicely.

Enjoy the Scandal Beck flowing beside you on your right and continue to its confluence with the River Eden. A narrow path, left, brings you to the long footbridge spanning the wide river.

In summer pause on the bridge and look for sandpipers flying low over the water to their territory along a pebbly part of the riverbank. Look downstream, where you might see a colony of sand martins. They constantly fly in to feed their ravenous young, which peer from their holes in the sandy river embankment. Coots nest here and swallows race just above the surface of the water after a myriad of flies that take to the wing at just the right time to provide food for their young.

Continue over the bridge and stroll on to the road to Warcop, the B6259. Cross with great care to continue ahead along Daleholme Lane for three-quarters of a mile towards Winton. Ahead, as you go, you have pleasing views across to Winton Fell, with its limestone scars and outcrops.

Cross with equal care the A685 and walk ahead into Winton. Turn left towards the centre of the village. On the green stands the

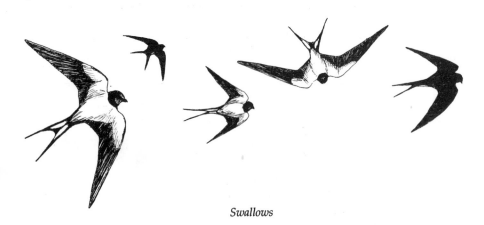

Swallows

elementary school, which dates from 1659. It was rebuilt in 1862 and was in use until 1977. Nearby is a fine three-storeyed dwelling, once a Dickensian-type boys school. Once in attendance the children were never allowed home until their education was finished in case they told how they were ill-treated.

Bear right to take the signposted lane to Hartley, passing in front of the Bay Horse inn. At the next Y-junction take the right branch to walk the narrow lane. After a quarter of a mile, turn left to stroll another byway. At its end, turn right and continue to the hamlet of Hartley Fold.

Here turn right, the road passing between the side walls of two huge barns. Beyond is a small green and a pretty white farmhouse made diminutive by the large buildings, now turned into separate lock-up units These old barns have been refurbished by the Rural Environment Commission.

To your left is Hartley Beck. Stroll beside it to take the signposted footbridge over the stream. Walk ahead across a large field, keeping beside the fence on your left. Pass through a kissing gate and swing right to cross Frank's Bridge over the River Eden. Walk on and almost immediately climb the steps on your right. Follow the walled way right and go on to pass the gateway to the church on your right. At the main street, cross, turn right and then left, following the road signs for the car park.

Walk 26: Ravenstonedale – Stennerskeugh Bridge

Ravenstonedale – Townhead Lane – Low Stennerskeugh – Stennerskeugh Bridge – Flass – Bowber Head – Low Lane – Ravenstonedale

Start/finish:	A large lay-by by the village school, which stands beside St Oswald's Church, 5 miles south of Kirkby Stephen (GR 724043).
Type of walk:	This delightful 5 to 6 mile walk passes through pastures, over moorland and alongside dancing becks. It surmounts a great number of limestone walls through which a team from the East Cumbria Countryside Project has constructed low step-stiles, each one gated and with a strong hook-and-eye catch. The route is well signposted.
Map:	OS Outdoor Leisure 19 Howgill Fells and Upper Eden Valley

The Walk

Leave the wide lay-by by the school and walk the A683, the road for Sedbergh, towards the main part of the village, with the Scandal Beck to your left. Pass on your right an art gallery and the Black Swan Hotel.

Follow the road round right, to go by the post office and the Wesleyan chapel (known as Low Chapel because of its position in the road). A short distance up the hill and opposite the United Reformed Church (known as High Chapel), take a small flight of signposted stone steps into a planting of trees. Bear left to pass through a waymarked kissing gate.

From now on the next nine easy-to-spot stiles take you over small pastures enclosed by pale-coloured limestone walls. As you go, enjoy the view of the surrounding hills, the scattered farms, the stone barns and the small copses of trees used for shelter.

After the last stile, cross Townhead Lane and pass through the stile opposite. Stride slightly left to the next one below a clump of ash. Go on in the same direction to the stile tucked into the right corner of the pasture, and then onto a stile to the access track to Row Foot Farm.

Turn right and after a few paces take the waymarked stile on the left. Beyond, bear right and carry on over the pasture, keeping parallel with the wall on your right. Cross a small ditch on a turf bridge and stroll on to a stile immediately to the left of Lockholme (meaning a water meadow) Farm. Cross its access track and take the stile opposite.

Walk ahead to the next stile and then join the track to the left of pretty Lockholme Hall Farm. Look for a plaque with the initials HF 1697 (the F for Fothergill, an important family in the dale in years gone by).

Saunter on to take the stile ahead, the farm track swinging away right. Walk on through a narrow, walled pasture. Beyond the next stile, drop downhill and climb a stile to pass to the left of Lockholme Head.

Press on ahead, as requested by a notice, with the wall to the right. Cross the tractor bridge over Ellergill Syke and then the next stile ahead. From here aim slightly left along a clear path to pass a waymark. Beyond, continue left to a stile in the wall edging the A683.

Cross with care to take the stile opposite. (Use your map for the next section of the walk.) Go ahead to pass through a signposted gate and walk diagonally right to a waymarked metal gate. Look ahead as you go, if in late summer, for a glorious view of purple heather on the slopes of Kirkby Stephen Common.

Continue towards Low Stennerskeugh (meaning wood near rocky ground) Farm and, just before a gateless gap, take the stile in the wall on the right. Stride on to the next stile, which is tucked up beside the farmhouse, now on your left.

Ignore the next stile on your left and stride ahead to a gate which comes into view as you move on away from the farm. The gate is in front of Stennerskeugh Farm. Turn left onto a road and where it divides, walk the continuing right fork. Pass through a gate and follow the track, using a clapper over a small stream – and a few boulders if the stream has flowed over the track.

Proceed along the track to cross the fine Stennerskeugh Bridge, once a packhorse bridge and part of the old highway. Stride the track, keeping beside the wall on your left. Do not continue along the track onto Flass Fell – a great temptation because the way is so pleasant – but follow the wall, using a narrow path that keeps beside it as it swings left to pass to the right of Flass Farm, where you join a narrow road.

Follow this pleasing way to cross the A683 to the right of South Bridge, Crooks Beck. Beyond, stroll the narrow lane, keeping to the

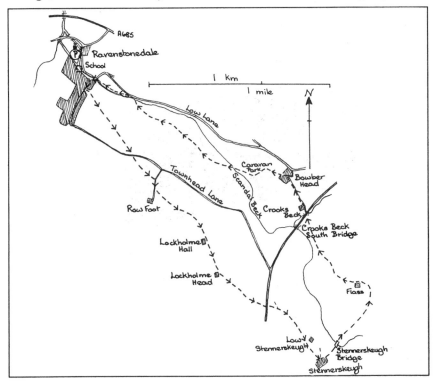

right of Crooks Beck Farm. At Bowber Head Farm, turn left through a small gate beside a cattle grid. Follow the track for 50 metres and turn left into a walled track before the start of a caravan park.

Drop downhill on a walled green trod to pass through a sturdy wooden gate. Head on, bearing right, to cross a footbridge over a small tributary stream. Go through the stile beyond. Continue on the same diagonal, heading away from the stream, to climb a stile in the top corner. Beyond, you are walking beside the Scandal Beck, on your left, once more.

From now on the well-stiled (eight stiles) path continues beside the beck. After climbing the last one, turn right to cross a bridge to Low Lane.

Turn left and after 45 metres take the waymarked path on the left, with the Scandal still to your left. This stiled path quickly brings you back to Ravenstonedale. Turn left and then right to return to your car.

Stennerskeugh Bridge

Walk 27: Ravenstonedale – Newbiggin-on-Lune

Ravenstonedale – Smardale Bridge – Smardale Gill viaduct – Dismantled railway – Brownber – Newbiggin-on-Lune – Ravenstonedale

Start/finish: The triangular-shaped lay-by by the phone box, close to the village school and beside St Oswald's Church (GR 723043). Ravenstonedale lies 5 miles south of Kirkby Stephen.

Type of walk: This delightful 6-mile walk takes you through the delectable countryside around the village. Easy walking all the way. Tranquil Ravenstonedale seems to have stood still for the last fifty years. It has charming stone houses and cottages which line both sides of a long, ascending street. It is often known as Town to distinguish it from the dale. Much of Town was built in about the 16th century, when Lord Wharton decided to create a deer park with 9 feet high walls, and moved any tenants in the way to poorer undrained land close to the Scandal Beck. It has a splendid church and a large churchyard dotted with magnificent conifers.

Map: OS Outdoor Leisure 19 Howgill Fells and Upper Eden Valley

The Walk

Start the walk with a visit to St Oswald's. In 1738 rebuilding of the church began, using much stone from an earlier derelict church. It was completed in 1744. Go inside and look for the splendid three-decker pulpit, taken from the old church, still with its inlaid sounding board – the vicar says that he feels vertiginous when he very occasionally uses the top deck.

The church's fine oak pews face each other across the central aisle, collegiate style. Look for the boards that display the Creed and the Lord's Prayer, both of which came from the original church. Two bells from the old church, with one dating from 1743, hang in the tower. The stained glass windows are very handsome. The one to the left of the altar depicts Eleanor Gaunt, martyred in 1686. Another shows St Oswald who died, aged 38, fighting the heathen King of Mercia. Opposite is another window showing St Aidan. This window was brought from the church at Newbiggin-on-Lune when it was closed.

As you leave, look in the porch for the 12th-century corbels, depicting the heads of wolves. Turn right out of the door and then right again to see the well-maintained Gilbertine ruins, part of a small monastic house or cell. Here lived three canons who dealt with religious and clerical matters, and several lay brothers who would have looked after the cell's farm, rabbits and fishponds.

Leave the churchyard by the double gates out into a pasture. Walk ahead to pass through two more gates to join a road. Turn left to stroll in the direction of the King's Head Inn. Cross the bridge over the Scandal Beck and take the signposted way for Smardale Bridge, on the opposite side of the road. A narrow tarmacked lane passes between cottages and then passes under the A685.

Leave the road, right, and continue on a narrow path beside the beck, keeping to the right side of Park House Farm. Pass through a waymarked gate and walk on to take an easy-to-miss marked stile in the wall on your left. Go on in the same general direction, steadily climbing left to join the farm access track. Leave the latter when it swings left and walk ahead over the pasture to a gap stile in the boundary wall. Beyond, bear slightly left and then climb a small hill ahead. Continue beside a fence and a small conifer plantation, both on your left, to a stile in the wall. To your right is a pleasing view of the beck and into Smardale Gill.

Continue ahead over a large pasture to a gap stile in the wall. Beyond, bear right to cross Smardale Bridge, traditionally known as County Bridge because it was maintained by the county. It was once part of the old route from Tebay to Brough, which predated the 1760

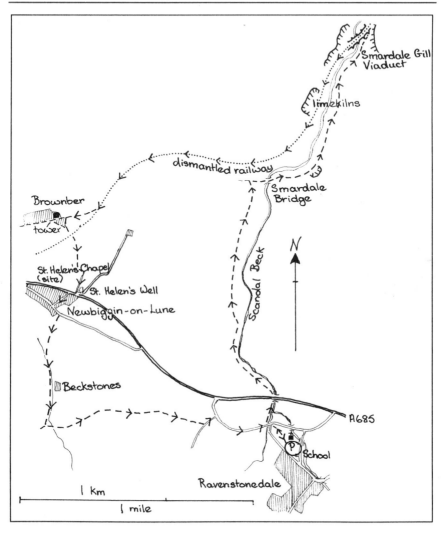

turnpike road nearby. Bear left uphill to cross a stile on the left. From here a splendid permissive grassy way, once an old quarry track, takes you on over glorious slopes to the far end of the 14-arched viaduct which spans the Smardale Gorge (walk 24). From here the views are spectacular but take care on the high narrow path as you near the bridge.

Climb the stile and turn left to cross the viaduct. It was built in

1860, part of the South Durham and Lancashire Union railway that carried coking coal from the north-east to ironworks in the west. It was restored by the Northern Viaduct Trust in 1992. Enjoy the dramatic view of the Howgills and the Lune Gorge and stride on to pass two huge limekilns. Look inside to see that each has two furnace holes. Railway wagons would have transported the lime.

As you walk the trackbed, look for the 'imprint' of the old sleepers. Go on along the gated trackbed, a veritable flower garden in summer months, and continue for nearly 2 miles from the viaduct to a short downward slope to join a farm track. Turn right to stroll past Brownber Farm. Beyond, on the right, is Tower House. This is where Elizabeth Gaunt, the woman depicted in stained glass in the church, was believed to have lived. She was born a Fothergill, one of the famous families in the dale. She gave help to all who asked. One who did was a wounded rebel from the 1685 Monmouth rebellion, whom she concealed in her house. When he heard that he could obtain indemnity and that there was a reward for betraying criminals, he 'shopped' Elizabeth. She was burnt at the stake at Tyburn in London in October 1685.

Opposite the tower, turn left to walk a wide, walled track which keeps to the right of the farm and leads to Newbiggin-on-Lune. Just before you reach the A685, turn left into a lane and stop. Look over the wall to see a long mound, believed to be the site of St Helen's chapel. Here too, shaded by quivering aspens, is St Helen's well. Some say it is the source of the River Lune because when all the source streams – Green Bell (walk 29), for example – dry up, this well still gives forth water. At least Newbiggin can claim to be the first village on the Lune.

Cross the busy road with care and continue past the aptly named Lune Spring garden centre and coffee shop into the village. Overlooking the green stands a private house, Aidans, that once was the village church of St Aidan's. Turn left to pass Bovil House, with the wall of its yard dramatically crenellated. Beyond, take the stile on the right, with the rounded rolling humps of the Howgills ahead. Stroll the long pasture, keeping beside the wall on the right. This brings you to a stone-stepped stile that gives access to a walled, railed path to come to the right of Beckstones Farm. Cross the beck by a footbridge on the right and continue along the tarmacked lane.

Once beyond the cattle grid, take the gate on the left and then the next gate on your left. Walk ahead to cross a footbridge and continue to the right of a barn. Climb the slope, with a derelict wall to your right. From now on the clear stiled and gated way continues across the high pastures, with majestic views to help you complete the walk.

At the narrow road turn left and at the T-junction turn right to cross the bridge. Walk on to pass the King's Head Inn. The footpath to the churchyard, and to rejoin your car, goes off right, beyond.

Limekilns, Smardale

Walk 28: Harter Fell and Little Harter Fell

Ravenstonedale – Town Head – Banks – Adamthwaite –
Harter Fell – Little Harter Fell – Paradise – Row Foot –
Piper Hole – Town Head

Start/finish:	A large lay-by by Ravenstonedale village school, which stands beside St Oswald's Church, 5 miles south of Kirkby Stephen (GR 24043).
Type of walk:	This 7-mile walk starts off along a pleasing narrow road, which climbs into the fells. It is a 'no through road' and you are likely to meet only farm vehicles. The walk continues on a glorious, shelf-like path, often muddy to begin with, but soon becoming sheer joy to walk. From it you have a bird's-eye view of the Rawthey valley and, close at hand, Adamthwaite Farm tucked into its tree-girt hollow. The splendid ridge walk is much too short, so make the most of every step. The return route, after a stretch on the narrow road again, lies across the quiet, stiled pastures south-east of Ravenstonedale – walked in the opposite direction on walk 26.
Map:	OS Outdoor Leisure 19 Howgill Fells and the Eden Valley

The Walk

From the parking area, walk south-east towards the centre of the village, upstream of the Scandal Beck, which lies on your left. Pass the galleried art gallery and the Black Swan Hotel.

Follow the road as it bears right to climb uphill between the grey stone houses. Go past the first green, which lies to your right, and continue on to the second at Town Head. Pass a small stone building, on your right, which once housed the village pig. All the folk fed it and they all ate it after it was slaughtered.

Continue towards the crossroads. Go over the Artlegarth Beck by an Irish bridge – a name given to similar bridges by Forest Enterprise in the Lake District. These bridges are built to allow water to flow both under and over the top when the beck is in spate. In May and June the banks of the hurrying stream are bright with cushions of kingcups, forget-me-nots and water avens.

Beyond the bridge bear left in the direction of Artlegarth and Adamthwaite. Away to your right lies Green Bell (walk 29), ahead is Harter Fell the object of this walk, and to the left looms Wild Boar Fell (walk 5).

Stride the long lane, ignoring the left turn for Artlegarth. Go on, gradually ascending to pass the pretty Banks farmhouse on your left. Beyond, rowan lean over the road and from these trees, in early spring, come the songs of willow warblers. Go on to pass a derelict barn on your left and a small quarry on your right. The latter would have supplied the stone for the walls and buildings.

After another small quarry, descend the road to cross a stone bridge over Gais Gill. The climb up from the bridge is very steep, so take your time. Watch for your first glimpse of Adamthwaite Farm, with Wandale Hill (walk 9) looming, large and shapely, behind it. At this point you can see the track along which this walk continues skirting the slopes of Harter Fell, on your left.

A dozen or more paces onward, when the farmhouse has disappeared from view, look for the grassy start of the track on your left. This is easy to miss. The track descends to a small ford over Stonely Gill, with its pretty waterfall to your right. Here you might be lucky to see a heron feeding. Beyond the ford the muddy track rapidly becomes a glorious grassy trod.

Pause to identify the fells about you; beyond Wandale and to its right is the long humpback of Kensgriff (walk 10). Above the latter is the long ridge leading from Randygill Top (walk 30) to Green Bell. Look to the left of Kensgriff for the huge gullies running down the east slopes of Yarlside (walk 10). Continue on the same contour to curve round the lower slopes of Harter Fell.

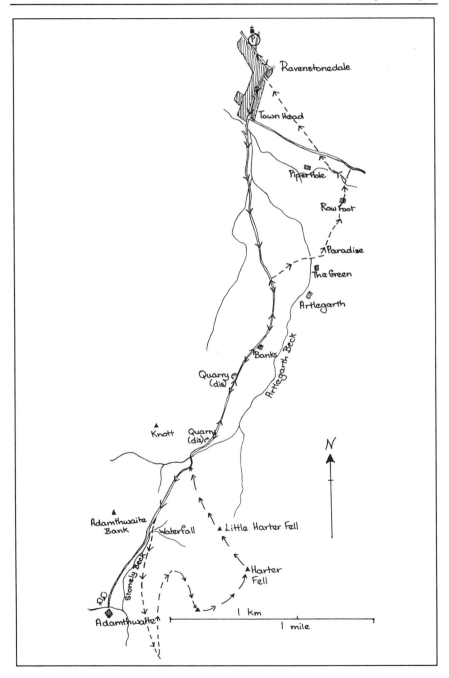

'Irish' Bridge, Ravenstonedale

Where the track comes right beside the wall coming in on your right, take a second track – deeply rutted by tractor wheels – that climbs obliquely left. As you ascend you might spot several black fell ponies grazing. Follow the track until it ceases in the mat grass. Ahead is a small gill through which flows Stonely Beck, crossed earlier far below.

Look for the continuing tractor marks, fainter and not rutted, as they wind right and upwards, with Stonely Gill always away to the left. Follow these to the highest point ahead at 1575ft (480m) and marked with a couple of stones. Pause here for a fine view of the Rawthey valley and a glimpse the A683 to Kirkby Stephen.

Look left to see the clear grassy track leading along the ridge towards Harter Fell. As you go, look down right to see Stennerskeugh and Fell End Clouds (walk 4), very white against the dark slopes of its Wild Boar parent. Then the small cairn on the fell ahead comes into view.

Dawdle on to the summit, 1709ft (521m), serenaded in spring by skylarks, and enjoy the magnificent 360 degrees view. Turn left (north-west, and with Fell End Clouds behind you) to leave the cairn, and at the rim of the tiny plateau you can see the cairn on Little Harter Fell, 1575ft (480m). The way is over the mat grass, with no path to help you. Keep to the higher ground for a quarter-of-a-mile stroll.

From the cairn you can see a small stretch of the narrow road taken earlier. Look about for the faint tractor marks and use this route to descend easily to the road, where you turn right. Drop down the steep slope to cross the bridge and then continue on to pass again, first Banks farmhouse and then the turning to Artlegarth. Just beyond a row of conifers and mixed deciduous trees, take the right turn, a track signposted The Green.

Continue beside the row of trees, with pasture to your left. Cross a small beck and then go through a gate to cross a second and walk on to the next gate. (To your right is The Green, which you ignore.) Follow the track as it swings left and continue parallel with the wall to your left.

On the right is a tarn and on the map this area is marked as Paradise. When the black headed gulls are nesting, all round the tarn and on small isthmuses and islands, for some walkers it will indeed be paradise. The noise of the gullery in spring is intense and there is a constant flying in and out and much aggression shown to crows who come seeking a meal of unattended eggs or fledglings. Tufted ducks, coots and geese with young are tolerated and these seem unperturbed by their noisy, numerous neighbours.

Water avens and kingcups

Follow the track to the wall ahead, and pass through the gap stile to the left of the gate. Walk on down the slope and pass between the yard and the farmhouse of Row Foot. Stride the walled track beyond (walk 26). Ignore the stile on the right and take the signposted gated stile on the left on the far side of Lockholme Beck.

Saunter on, with the beck to your left, to take the next gated stile. Walk on to pass Piper Hole, a deep depression on your left, to take a stile, slightly right, in the fence ahead. Carry on to a stepped stile to a narrow lane. Cross and take the stepped stile opposite. Look left for the first of the seven stiles, all well-signposted and maintained, that take you back across the pleasing pastures to a kissing gate into a copse of trees. Follow the path that leads through the conifers to steps which you descend to join the main street of Ravenstonedale, opposite the United Reformed Church.

Turn right and follow the road round left to rejoin your car. Visit the church and the Gilbertine ruins if you have not been able to before (see walk 26).

Walk 29: Ravenstonedale – Green Bell

Ravenstonedale – Town Head – Philip Close – Wyegarth
Gill – Knoutberry – Green Bell 1985 ft (605m) – Hunthoof
Pike – Low Knott – Weasdale Lane – Greenside – Town
Head

Start/finish: The triangular-shaped lay-by close to the phone
box by Ravenstonedale village school (GR
723042). The village lies 5 miles south of Kirkby
Stephen.

Type of walk: There are no very clear footpaths, no signposts
and no arrows to help you on this glorious 7-mile
circular walk to the summit of Green Bell. A long,
steady climb takes you to the top, which is in view
for most of the way. The start is along a cart track,
which can be muddy after rain. Care should be
exercised to avoid the marshy areas (where red
grass and bright green moss indicate sponginess).
Once you reach the faint grooved path up to
Knoutberry and on along the tops, the walking is
very pleasant indeed. The return from the summit
is down a wide grassy track, and then a cart track,
to join a narrow lane. The walk from the outskirts
of Newbiggin-on-Lune to Ravenstonedale is along
unsignposted rights of way over pleasing pastures.

Map: OS Outdoor Leisure 19 Howgill Fells and Upper
Eden Valley

The Walk

Green Bell is one of the steep-sided, softly domed northern fells. The
view from the trig point is spectacular. From it you can see the
Lakeland fells, the other Howgills, the tops of some of the Yorkshire
fells and a very long stretch of the Cross Fell range. Below you can

see the buildings of Ravenstonedale and Newbiggin-on-Lune nestling among trees, and the River Lune journeying on its way through pastures to the Crook of Lune. The source of this splendid river, sometimes a mere trickle, is below the old sheepfold just before you climb to the summit of Green Bell.

Start the walk from the parking area and go south, with the Scandal Beck to your left. Pass the art gallery and then the Black Swan Hotel. Follow the road round right and climb uphill, passing between the delightful cottages and houses. Look for the Wesleyan chapel on the left and then the United Reformed Church on the right. Pass the first village green, also on the right, to continue to another at Town Head. Pass the small building on the green where the villagers once kept a pig.

Continue on and bear right to cross a stone bridge. Beyond, turn right and walk to the left of two wooden bridges to cross Lockholme Beck where it unites with Wyegarth Gill. Go on along the continuing farm track. Pass through the gate and go on along the track, with walls to either side. Continue on the track when the wall turns away right. Carry on, still with a wall to the left, along the grass and stone track.

Stroll on to pass the walled enclosure of Philip Close and then, as the track disappears, move left towards the edge of the shallow Wraygill. Look right to see a boggy area and, uphill, slightly right, to see a grooved path.

Continue along the side of the gill and once past the mire, head upwards to join the grooved way that leads steadily, right, towards Knoutberry 1736 ft (529m). From now on the grassy way leads to the small summit and then over a saddle to the foot of Green Bell, where you might disturb roe deer grazing. Look for the old sheepfold and close to it, the highest of the source springs of the River Lune.

A clear, wide grassy track leads straight up to a small flat area, a nice place for a pause. And then go on climbing to the summit, still on a good track. Stride across the almost level top and pause beside the trig point to enjoy the incredible view.

Leave the top by another wide track (in the direction of Newbiggin-on-Lune) which runs north. It is west of the route by which you

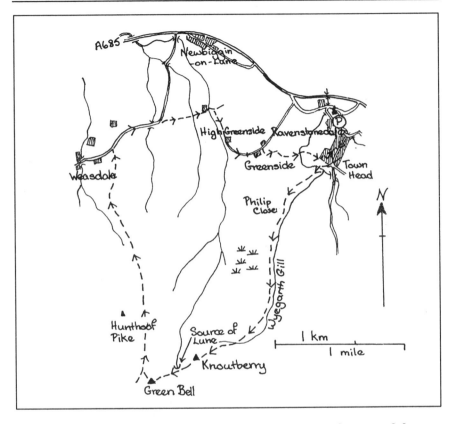

approached the summit. Keep to the track as it goes down and down, easily and a pleasure to stroll. It passes on the left Hunthoof Pike, 1719 ft (524m), with just a clump of stones for a cairn. Continue towards a walled pasture above Weasdale. By the wall, now on your left, a good cart track continues all the way to the road to Weasdale, where you turn right.

As you go look for fell ponies, some a rich dark brown and others piebald. Where the road swings left towards Newbiggin, go on ahead until you reach a gate on the right (walk 27). Pass through and take a few steps to go through the next one on the left. Stride on ahead to cross Greenside Beck. Walk on to the fine barn on your left. Go through the gate in the wall on your right.

Saunter on, keeping to the left of some lofty sycamores. From here

Fell pony and foal

you have a good view of Green Bell. Go through a gate ahead and then on to take a gate on the left, just before High Greenside, onto a gated track. This leads through the farm buildings and onto first the access track and then a narrow road, along which you continue.

Walk the delightful lane, with Wild Boar Fell (walk 5) and Stenneskeugh Clouds (walk 4) ahead. Once over the cattle grid at Greenside, pass one dwelling and take a gate on the right, below a telegraph pole and immediately before the next house. (As the book went to press there was a plot for sale between the two dwellings.) The gate gives access to a tiny, manicured lawn, which you leave by another gate. Go left through a gate in the wall and then drop down the pasture to a narrow stile in the right corner. Turn left and walk beside the wall on the left to pass through two gateless gaps.

Beyond the second one, turn right and descend to a broken stile in the wall. Once over, and with the wall to your right, go on to pass through a gate. Follow the track to cross a charming stone bridge over an almost dry beck. Pass through the next gate and strike diagonally left to join a track to Town Head Farm. Follow the track and where it bears right, pass through a series of gates to walk to the green with the stone building, once the pig sty. Turn left and walk downhill through the village and bear left to rejoin your car.

Walk 30: Hooksey – Randygill Top – Green Bell

A685 – Hooksey – Leathgill Bridge – Randygill Top –
Stockless – Green Bell – Weasdale – A685

Start/finish: A grassy verge close to Brow Foot (GR 686049).
Leave the A685 at the well-signposted turn for
Bowderdale and follow the narrow road as it
swings right. Where it turns left, away from the
A-road, park on the verge on the right, well away
from a gate to a pasture.

Type of walk: This is a magnificent 7½ miler, with glorious views
from the several tops. Tracks and a short path
make finding the way easy, allowing you to enjoy
to the full the springy turf, the generally steady
gradients (one short stiff climb) and the birdlife,
and to imbibe the grandness of the Howgills. As
you come to know the fells, by building up your
walks, they become addictive. It is a delight to look
down on, or up to, the area where you walked on
another glorious day's excursion. This walk, in
good weather, presents no problems.

Map: OS Outdoor Leisure 19 Howgill Fells and the Upper Eden Valley

The Walk

From the parking lay-by, walk on to take the first left turn, ignoring
the right turn for Bowderdale (taken for walk 31). Where the narrow
road swings left to Scar Sikes, go ahead on the continuing farm track.
Here in spring and early summer you are likely to hear and see
curlews, redshanks, snipe and green plovers.

Continue on the gated way. To your right towers West Fell (walk

31) and to the left are the lower slopes of Hooksey. Where the track divides, ignore the one that turns right, following the wall, and stride the track that carries on ahead. Press on the pleasing grassy trod, which is well marked with tractor wheels, as it climbs steadily. Look out for the small wall on your right, most likely con-structed to give shel-ter for the sheep. It is marked on the OS map.

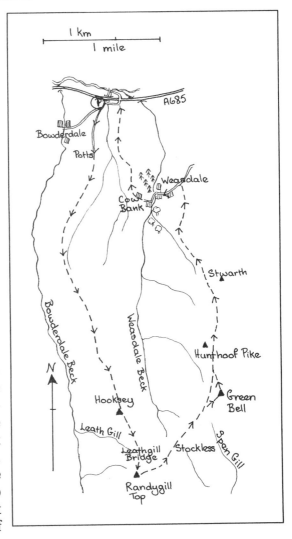

Follow the track up onto the extensive ridge, where it be-comes almost as wide as a road, but is not eroded in any way. Look ahead to the right of Randygill Top to see Hazelgill Knott and the great bulk of Yarlside. And then, just before the now grassy way begins to descend, stand by the tiny summit cairn, 1923ft (586m), composed of a few stones.

Descend the continuing track to cross Leathgill Bridge – not a real bridge but a rounded high saddle between Hooksey and Randygill Top. Ahead is the short steep climb to the summit, out of view at this point in the walk but seen earlier from the top of Hooksey. The way up starts with tractor wheels marking the route and then it continues as a narrow path that leads to the cairn, 2034ft (620 m). See how many tops in the Howgills, Lakeland, the Pennines and Yorkshire you can spot.

Turn left to begin one of the best ridge walks in the Howgills. It stretches away, wide and springy, over Stockless, 1864ft (568m), and then on through a grooved trod onto Green Bell, 1985ft (605m), with its trig point standing out clearly. From this top you have a spectacular view of Yarlside, Randygill Top and The Calf.

Hooksey and Randygill Top

From the cairn, bear left (north), as for walk 29, to stride a clear, green track heading from the summit towards the Lune valley and, in particular, the wooded hamlet of Weasdale. Look north-east to see the Smardale Gill viaduct. At a crossing of tracks, stride ahead, ignoring the left and right turns. Go on down to the next crossing and do the same. This brings you close to a wall on the left to stride a rough farm track. Go on with several enclosures to your left to join a narrow road.

Turn left to pass a derelict farmhouse and then continue to the T-junction. Turn left again to pass in front of Weasdale farmhouse and walk the road to stand on the bridge over Weasdale Beck. Here the lively stream hurries round boulders and trees shade the water, a corner contrasting sharply with the grassy fells above.

Stroll on along the road as it swings right and becomes edged, on the right, with conifers and rowan. Pass the derelict Cow Bank farmhouse and go on the continuing farm track.

Stride on to a gate, and beyond the track passes through a pasture to another. If there has been much rain and the cattle have used the pasture, this can be a rather wet way. Beyond this second gate, the track improves and goes on as a walled green way.

Follow the clear, grassy track as it passes through pastures to a gate to a lane Beyond stroll the delightful way, its verges a blaze of deep pink, in late spring, where water avens thrive in great clumps. At the lane end turn left to return to your car.

Redshank

```
┌─────────────────────────────────────────────────┐
│ ═══════════════════════════════════════════════ │
│                                                   │
│          Walk 31: Bowderdale                      │
│                                                   │
│ ═══════════════════════════════════════════════ │
└─────────────────────────────────────────────────┘
```

Walk 31: Bowderdale

Brow Foot – Bowderdale Head – West Fell – Hazelgill
Knott – Bowderdale Beck – Brow Foot

Start/finish:	A grassy verge close to Brow Foot (GR 686049). Leave the A685 at the well-signposted turn for Bowderdale and follow the narrow road as it swings right. Where it turns left, away from the A-road, park on the verge on the right, well away from a gate to a pasture.
Type of walk:	This exhilarating 8½ mile walk takes you along the glorious ridge of West Fell and over Hazelgill Knott. After an exciting descent just beyond Hazel Gill the return is made through Bowderdale, striding the bridleway, an airy path that keeps above the Bowderdale Beck. Do the walk in late spring when the air is filled with the songs of meadow pipits and skylarks and the evocative calls of curlews. This is not a walk for rainy or misty weather.
Map:	OS Outdoor Leisure 19 Howgill Fells and Upper Eden Valley

The Walk

From the grassy verge, walk on along the narrow road, ignoring the left turn for Potts (the way you return). Follow the sign, high on a telegraph pole, for Bowderdale. In spring you might see green plovers perform their aerial, acrobatic, courting rituals, accompanied by musical whistles, over the fields around the hamlet.

Notice the charming Bowderdale Foot farmhouse, where swallows return each spring. Nearby, the beck is edged by sweet-smelling gorse. Climb the short hill and then leave the road to take the bridlepath, signposted Bowderdale, on the left. After heavy rain

choose the drier way
and walk the continu-
ing track, with a wall to
your right.

Pass a planting of
conifers on your right,
where small tortoise-
shell butterflies flit
along the verge. Go on
the gated way, now
with a larch plantation
to the left. Look for a
pair of buzzards that

Small tortoiseshell butterfly

can often be seen riding the thermals above the trees.

Aim for the gate in the top right corner of the fell wall. Once
through continue on the good track beside the wall on your left. At
the corner, where the wall turns away and descends (and the place
to which you should return if the beck is unfordable), leave the track
and begin the steady climb up the slopes on a grassy tractor route.

This delightful way takes you steadily to the top of the uncairned
West Fell,1778 ft (542m). As you climb, pause often and enjoy the
retrospective view of the Lune valley, with its many limestone-
walled enclosures and clumps of trees. To the right as you ascend,

Yarlside and Bowderdale

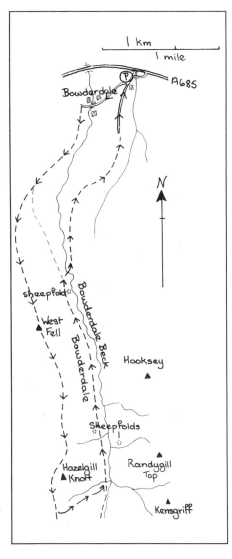

and far below, you can see the Langdale Beck snaking between its enfolding slopes.

Beyond the rather featureless summit continue, gently descending to a flat area just before the start of two paths that ascend Hazelgill Knott 1896ft (578m). The Knott is not rugged as its name suggests but a lovely, swelling grassy mound. The path to the right climbs steadily, winding round the fell, and gives you wonderful views into the lonely northern sides of the southern fells, with Yarlside dominating all.

After you have passed Hazel Gill on your left, leave the grassy trod and cross over left until you can look down into Bowderdale. There in no path for your descent and the best way down is by the spur just south of the gill. As you go, look right for a glimpse of the pastures about Cautley.

Join the bridlepath and turn left to walk below Randygill Top and then Hooksey (walk 30) on your right. The boulders on the fell slopes and about the beck are just right for wheatears to nest in crevices. To help you identify them as they flit from rock to rock, look for their white rumps.

Continue on the pleasing way for nearly 1½ miles from the foot of the Hazel Gill, until you see a sheepfold on the far side of the beck. If the stream is low cross on boulders and join a track – seen clearly from the bridlepath – steadily climbing upwards. If you cannot cross the beck or do not wish to wade, remain on the bridlepath until you reach the wall corner passed on your ascent of West Fell. From here retrace your outward route along the cart track to the hamlet and turn right to walk the narrow road.

If you can cross, continue on what soon becomes a wide clear track. As you reach a wall, bear right and stride on to join a metalled road, where you turn left. Ignore the right turn to Scar Sikes and continue to the junction passed at the outset. Bear right to rejoin your car close to the A685.

Walk 32: Langdale to Blakethwaite Bottom and Hand Lake

Langdale – Cowbound Lane (track) – Uldale Beck –
Blakethwaite Bottom – Hand Lake – Cowbound Lane –
Langdale

Start/finish: A large parking area to the west of the Lune Valley
Service Station in the hamlet of Gaisgill on the
A685. The proprietor invites you to park close to
the large tyres used as flower pots near to the
A-road, out of the way of lorries that use this
space for parking (GR 639054).

Type of walk: This is a challenging 8-mile walk. It would start in
a more satisfactory way if you could ascend by
Ellergill, but this would mean walking along a private path. It is a walk of much contrast. It takes
you over rough pastures, through birch woodland
beside a pretty beck and across a charming packhorse bridge. It continues along an airy path above
the Uldale Beck, dallies in a remote hollow in the
heart of the Howgills and ascends and descends a
pathless fell. You have two becks to wade, boulder
hop or paddle – be warned.

Map: OS Outdoor Leisure 19 Howgill Fells and Upper
Eden Valley

The Walk

Leave the parking area to join and turn left along the narrow lane
through the hamlet of Gaisgill. Follow the signpost for Langdale –
both the map and the signpost say Longdale and that is just what it
is.

Stride the quiet, hedged lane for a quarter-of-a-mile, crossing bridges over Ellergill Beck and Langdale Beck. Pass the old school on the left and walk on to take, on the left, a wide, walled outrake named Cowbound Lane. After rain the track – for that is what it is – becomes very muddy. It soon turns right and climbs quite steeply to come beside a plantation of conifers on your left.

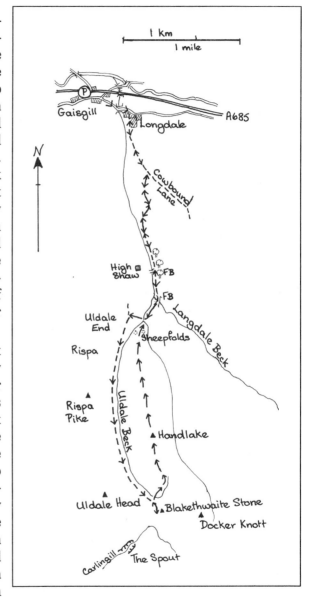

When the right wall turns away right, follow it over pasture that is rough underfoot where cattle have puddled. Continue with the wall to your right, choosing the driest way to pass, first, the remnants of a sheepfold and then, further on, a fine bank barn on your right.

Stroll on to the second gate in the wall beyond the barn. This has an awkward catch and lies at the point where three walls meet, just after you have walked for half-a-mile from the plantation.

Beyond the gate there is little evidence of a track but walk ahead, in the same general direction, descending slightly, to join an excellent track. This is a great delight to walk as it drops steadily towards deciduous woodland about the Langdale Beck. In June wood sorrel and primroses thrive below the birch that covers the steep slopes. Continue beside the beck, its chuckling waters edged with ash.

Packhorse Bridge, Langdale

Pass a charming packhorse bridge, which would once have been used by the people who lived at High Shaw, a derelict but still picturesque farmhouse. Leave the trees and stride on to climb a difficult stile over the boundary wall.

Just beyond is another delightful packhorse bridge spanning the Langdale Beck. Pause here and look for the water-smoothed boulders beneath it. Once you have crossed the bridge, you will see to your right the Uldale Beck flowing into the Langdale. A few paces along the Uldale is a ford, on your right, which you should cross by boulder hopping or wading.

Continue upstream, remaining beside the hurrying beck on your left, with a wall to your right. From here you can look left into Churn Gill, which divides Middleton Fell and Hand Lake Fell, the latter your return route.

Where the wall turns right and climbs the slope to Uldale End you have a choice of routes – you can continue beside the beck on sheep trods or climb the steep slope to join a good path that runs high above the dale. Its start is to be found at the point where the wall turns away right once more. This is a glorious high-level path (there is an even higher one) that gives you a grand view of the beck meandering through its valley.

After three-quarters-of-a-mile the path steadily descends towards a sheepfold and goes on much closer to the Uldale. If you have remained beside the beck this is where you will join the continuing good path.

Stroll on into Uldale, where on a sunny midsummer morning you have the sun full on your face. To your left are the steep slopes of Hand Lake and to your right is Rispa Pike and then Uldale Head (walk 19).

The pleasant path leads you into a wide, green, level amphitheatre, known as Blakethwaite Bottom. As the path bears right across the glorious hollow, look for the boulder on your left. This is large and pitted, scored with faint initials and a benchmark. It is surrounded by rushes and it marks the old boundary between Westmorland and Yorkshire.

Follow the path across the grassy flat, with Docker Knott to your left, to reach the side of Great Ulgill Beck, dancing through its pleasant gill – this is the place for your picnic.

Return across Blakethwaite Bottom and cross the head of Uldale to begin your climb up Hand Lake. To do this follow the tractor marks that climb up to the left of the rush-lined gill between the fell and Docker Knott. As you climb bear slightly left and as you go you can see the hollow of Churn Gill and then Langdale Gill come into view on your right.

The way to the top is pathless, so aim for the higher slopes all the time. The summit cairn, 1624ft (495m), is composed of ten small stones. Continue ahead, steadily descending, picking your way around the few peaty pools and peat hags. As you go, pause often to enjoy the magnificent views of the Lakeland fells, the Pennines and the Upper Eden valley.

Keep going down the trackless fell to come to an old sheepfold and a sheepwash by the confluence of Churngill Beck with Uldale Beck. Cross on boulders or wade Churngill Beck, which lies to your right. Climb the slope ahead and then continue left on the low, truncated spurs to join a track that goes on down to the packhorse bridge crossed earlier.

Beyond, turn left to climb the awkward stile and go along the pleasant gated path through the small woodland beside the Langdale Beck. Once through the gate, climb the continuing track, with a delightful view of pretty Langdale ahead. Where the track fades head for the gate in the wall corner. Turn left and follow the wall on your left to reach Cowbound Lane, which you descend to the hamlet of Langdale. Re-walk the narrow road for a quarter-of-a-mile to rejoin your car.

Boundary stone, Blakethwaite Bottom

More walking guides from:

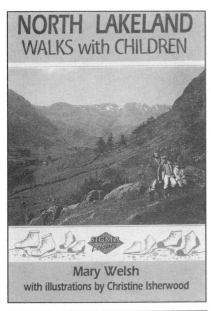

NORTH LAKELAND
WALKS with CHILDREN

Mary Welsh
with illustrations by Christine Isherwood

TEA SHOP WALKS in the *LAKE DISTRICT*

Jean Patefield

Also by Mary Welsh:

NORTH LAKELAND WALKS WITH CHILDREN
Mary Welsh
£6.95

COUNTRY WALKS AROUND KENDAL
Mary Welsh
£6.95

From other Sigma Leisure authors:

SOUTH LAKELAND WALKS WITH CHILDREN
Nick Lambert
£6.95

WALKING LAKELAND TRACKWAYS: the Eastern Lakes
Mike Cresswell
£6.95

TEA SHOP WALKS IN CUMBRIA & THE LAKE DISTRICT *(NEW!)*
June & Norman Buckley
£6.95

TEA SHOP WALKS IN THE LAKE DISTRICT
Jean Patefield
£6.95

THE LAKELAND SUMMITS: a survey of the fells of the Lake District National Park
Tim Synge
£7.95

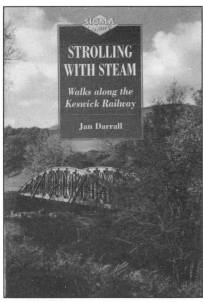

FULL DAYS ON THE LAKELAND FELLS:
25 challenging walks in the Lake District
Adrian Dixon
£7.95

STROLLING WITH STEAM:
Walks along the Keswick Railway
Jan Darrall
£4.95

100 LAKE DISTRICT HILL WALKS
Gordon Brown
£7.95

LAKELAND WALKING: on the level
Norman Buckley
£6.95

MOSTLY DOWNHILL: Leisurely Walks in the Lake District
Alan Pears
£6.95

LAKELAND ROCKY RAMBLES:
Geology beneath your feet
Bryan Lynas
£9.95

PUB WALKS IN THE LAKE DISTRICT
Neil Coates
£6.95

TOWN & VILLAGE DISCOVERY TRAILS: Cumbria & The Lake District
Norman Buckley
£6.95

In case of difficulty, or for a free catalogue, please contact: **SIGMA LEISURE, 1 SOUTH OAK LANE, WILMSLOW, CHESHIRE SK9 6AR.** Phone: 01625-531035; Fax: 01625-536800. E-mail: sigma.press@zetnet.co.uk . Web site: http//www.sigmapress.co.uk

ACCESS and VISA orders welcome. Please add £2 p&p to all orders.